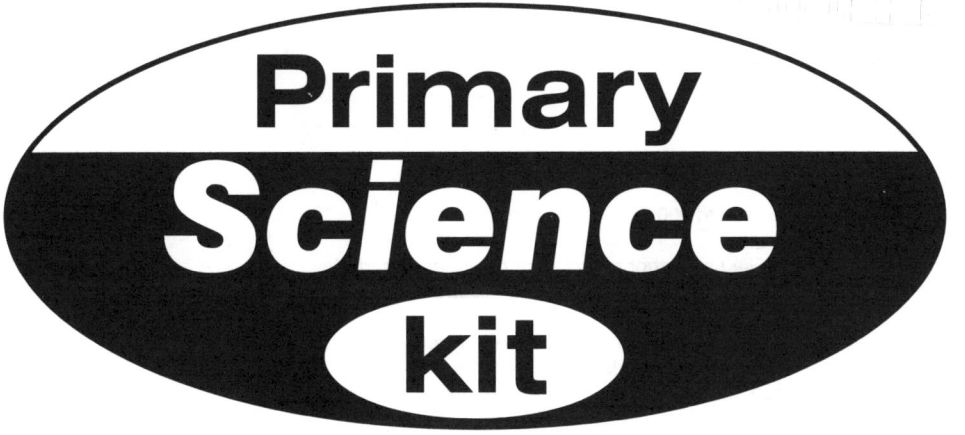

Science Assessment
Years 5–6

Lawrie Ryan

Text © Lawrie Ryan 2002
Original illustrations © Nelson Thornes Ltd 2002

The right of Lawrie Ryan to be identified as author of this work has been asserted by him in accordance with the Copyright, Designs and Patents Act 1988.

All rights reserved. No part of this publication may be reproduced or transmitted in any form or by any means, electronic or mechanical, including photocopy, recording or any information storage and retrieval system, without permission in writing from the publisher or under licence from the Copyright Licensing Agency Limited, of 90 Tottenham Court Road, London W1T 4LP.

Any person who commits any unauthorised act in relation to this publication may be liable to criminal prosecution and civil claims for damages.

Published in 2002 by:
NelsonThornes Ltd
Delta Place
27 Bath Road
CHELTENHAM
GL53 7TH
United Kingdom

02 03 04 05 06/ 10 9 8 7 6 5 4 3 2 1

A catalogue record for this book is available from the British Library

ISBN 0-7487-6863-7

Illustrations by Art Construction, IFA Design, Bethan Matthews, David Woodroffe
Page make-up by AMR

Printed and bound in Great Britain by Ashford Colour Press

CONTENTS

5A Keeping healthy
Pupil checklist (record of achievement) 6
End-of-unit assessment questions 7
Mark scheme for assessment questions 16
Teacher assessment recording sheet 17
Concept map 18
Complete the diagram 19

5B Life cycles
Pupil checklist (record of achievement) 20
End-of-unit Assessment questions 21
Mark scheme for assessment questions 26
Teacher assessment recording sheet 27
Concept map 28
Anagrams 29

5C Gases around us
Pupil checklist (record of achievement) 30
End-of-unit assessment questions 31
Mark scheme for assessment questions 37
Teacher assessment recording sheet 38
Concept map 39
Complete the diagram 40

5D Changing state
Pupil checklist (record of achievement) 41
End-of-unit assessment questions 42
Mark scheme for assessment questions 48
Teacher assessment recording sheet 49
Concept map 50

5E Earth, Sun and Moon
Pupil checklist (record of achievement) 51
End-of-unit assessment questions 52
Mark scheme for assessment questions 55
Teacher assessment recording sheet 56
Concept map 57
Concept cartoon 58

5F Changing sounds
Pupil checklist (record of achievement) 59
End-of-unit assessment questions 60
Mark scheme for assessment questions 64
Teacher assessment recording sheet 65
Concept map 66
Complete the diagram 67

End of Year 5 assessment
End-of-year assessment questions 68
Mark scheme for assessment questions 74

6A Plants and animals in the environment
Pupil checklist (record of achievement) 75
End-of-unit assessment questions 76
Mark scheme for assessment questions 82
Teacher assessment recording sheet 83
Concept map 84
Complete the diagram 85

6B Micro-organisms
Pupil checklist (record of achievement) 86
End-of-unit assessment questions 87
Mark scheme for assessment questions 91
Teacher assessment recording sheet 92
Concept map 93

6C More about dissolving
Pupil checklist (record of achievement) 94
End-of-unit assessment questions 95
Mark scheme for assessment questions 99
Teacher assessment recording sheet 100
Concept map 101

6D Reversible and irreversible changes
Pupil checklist (record of achievement) 102
End-of-unit assessment questions 103
Mark scheme for assessment questions 107
Teacher assessment recording sheet 108
Concept map 109

6E Forces in action
Pupil checklist (record of achievement) 110
End-of-unit assessment questions 111
Mark scheme for assessment questions 115
Teacher assessment recording sheet 116
Concept map 117
Concept cartoon 118

6F How we see things
Pupil checklist (record of achievement) 119
End-of-unit assessment questions 120
Mark scheme for assessment questions 124
Teacher assessment recording sheet 125
Concept map 126
Complete the diagram 127

6G Changing circuits
Pupil checklist (record of achievement) 128
End-of-unit assessment questions 129
Mark scheme for assessment questions 132
Teacher assessment recording sheet 133
Concept map 134

End of Year 6 Assessment
End-of-year assessment questions 135
Mark scheme for assessment questions 142

Summary sheet: KS2 teacher assessment 143
Continuation sheet: teacher assessment 144

Science Assessment Y5/6   © Lawrie Ryan, Nelson Thornes Ltd. 2002

GUIDANCE ON USING THIS RESOURCE

Introduction

This pack contains a variety of assessment resources, designed to be used flexibly. The materials are divided into units that correspond to the QCA Scheme of Work for Science in Years 5 and 6. (A separate pack is available for Years 3 and 4.)

For each unit, there is:
- a pupil checklist to provide a record of achievement
- an end-of-unit test that assesses progress against the learning outcomes stated in the QCA Scheme of Work
- an associated mark scheme
- teacher assessment recording sheets
- a variety of other assessment materials, such as pre-unit questions, concept maps and cartoons, or annotated drawings for children to reveal their thinking

There are also end-of-year tests and mark schemes.

Record of achievement pupil checklists

A crucial part of teaching is sharing your learning objectives with children. The record of achievement checklists will help you to do this. Learning objectives from the QCA Scheme of Work have been rewritten in terms that the children will understand. They are presented in knowledge-based and skill-based lists for children to tick off as they achieve each objective in class. Ideally, you should refer to the sheet at the start of the science session to share your learning objectives, then again at the end of the session for children to assess their progress. The checklists provide diagnostic assessment information and encourage useful discussion between teacher and child.

The sheets themselves offer a record of work covered in a unit and can therefore be a useful revision tool for children at the end of Key Stage 2, or if you choose to do an end-of-unit or end-of-year assessment.

Assessment questions

These questions are intended to assess the knowledge and understanding children gain in Sc2, 3 and 4 and relate closely to the learning outcomes in the QCA Scheme of Work. Many of the questions also enable children to demonstrate aspects of the Programme of Study for Sc1. This is consistent with the greater emphasis on Sc1-type questions now evident in the end-of-Key Stage 2 tests.

All the assessment questions have associated **mark schemes**.

Using these questions enables teachers to monitor children's progress formally throughout the year in science (as end-of-unit tests) or to gain summative assessment information (as end-of-year tests). Keeping records of class scores year on year will help schools compare the standards of different year groups objectively.

You can use the assessment questions flexibly by:
- omitting questions on topics that you have not covered in that unit
- mixing and matching questions from different units to customise assessment tests to your own scheme of work if it differs markedly from the QCA Scheme
- modifying questions to differentiate and meet the needs of your class or individuals with special educational needs at either end of the attainment spectrum
- selecting questions from the assessment test to tackle **during** the unit. These can be used as extension work for groups, as homework or for cover work for absent staff. It could be argued that using the questions in this way makes it easier for teachers to address pupil weaknesses they reveal, and for children to respond to feedback, hence providing useful **formative** assessment information.

Science Assessment Y5/6   © Lawrie Ryan, Nelson Thornes Ltd. 2002

GUIDANCE ON USING THIS RESOURCE

Teacher assessment recording sheets

Schools have always found that deciding how to record children's progress in science can be a thorny issue, but with the publication of the QCA Scheme of Work came the guidance quoted below.

> Learning outcomes in each unit show how children might demonstrate what they have learnt. The learning outcomes themselves will serve as a good record for classes working on each unit. It is not necessary to make detailed records for each child in relation to these outcomes. The end of unit expectations provide broad descriptions of achievement within each unit and should help teachers decide where a child's progress differs markedly from that of the rest of the class. Teachers may wish to make a note of this, and of the reasons for the difference, to pass on to the next teacher.
>
> The end of unit expectations are closely related to the level descriptions. When teachers come to end-of-key-stage judgements they should continue to refer to the level descriptions. Records of where a child's progress differs from the expectations for most children should assist this process.

In line with this guidance, the teacher assessment record sheets at the end of each unit offer a format that is quick and easy to use. As an alternative, at the end of each year's work, there is a single summary sheet to cover the whole of the Key Stage. As QCA recommend, the assessments will be a matter of professional judgement, informed by many sources of evidence (not necessarily recorded!). The resources in this pack will help in this process.

Other assessment material

Concept maps

These provide key words and ask the children to show the links between them, labelling their links to explain the connection. Once you have modelled the technique with a simple example, children can draw their own concept maps. These can give insight into how children are thinking, and will often prompt you to ask appropriate questions and seek clarification from individuals.

You could use concept maps before teaching a topic, to assess prior knowledge and understanding, or at the end of a topic. The technique has been used for self-assessment when children compare the concept map they draw before the topic to the one they produce after the topic. At the end of the topic, they will often see many more links than they were aware of at the start of the topic.

Concept cartoons

These are intended to provoke discussion and elicit children's ideas in an informal way. Cartoon characters are used to put forward ideas that children, in groups, discuss and decide which they agree with. The technique is often used to start investigative work, and yields excellent assessment information. It is particularly useful for those who have difficulty expressing themselves in writing.

The original idea of concept cartoons was put forward by Brenda Keogh and Stuart Naylor and their publications are available from Millgate House Publishers, Millgate House, 30 Mill Hill Lane, Sandbach, Cheshire CW11 4NP.

Annotated drawings

These can give teachers valuable insights into children's thinking. Discussion of the drawings afterwards is an excellent teaching/learning opportunity.

All these techniques give teachers a chance to respond to the assessments made and help children make progress in their scientific understanding.

Science Assessment Y5/6   © Lawrie Ryan, Nelson Thornes Ltd. 2002

KEEPING HEALTHY

Pupil checklist

By the end of this unit:

I should know that:

- [ ] a scientific idea can be tested and the evidence collected can support the idea or not
- [ ] to stay healthy I need to eat enough food and follow a balanced diet
- [ ] I need to exercise my muscles to stay fit and healthy
- [ ] when I exercise, I work harder
- [ ] my heart and lungs are protected by my ribs
- [ ] the muscle in the wall of my heart contracts regularly as it pumps blood around my body
- [ ] blood vessels carry blood around my body
- [ ] my muscles move parts of my skeleton and to do this my muscles need more blood to reach them, so my heart beats faster (and my pulse rate increases)
- [ ] drugs affect the way our bodies work
- [ ] tobacco and alcohol are examples of drugs that can have harmful effects on our bodies
- [ ] medicines are drugs that usually do us good, but can have side effects (especially if we don't follow the instructions about how much to take).

I should be able to:

- [ ] present information about diet and health
- [ ] measure pulse rate, repeating my measurements to make them more reliable
- [ ] draw a bar chart showing resting pulse rates and explain what it shows
- [ ] suggest some factors that might affect pulse rate
- [ ] make a prediction about how changing a factor affects pulse rate
- [ ] decide how many measurements of pulse rate we need and how many people to test
- [ ] present results on a line graph, explaining what they show and whether they support my prediction.

Science Assessment Y5/6   © Lawrie Ryan, Nelson Thornes Ltd. 2002

KEEPING HEALTHY

Assessment questions

Name .... Class .... Date ....

1 a)

> In the 18th century, doctors in Paris noticed that babies from richer families seemed more likely to die than babies from poor families. They looked at the diets of the babies. One thing they noticed was that rich families gave their babies milk that had been boiled, but the poor families didn't boil their milk.

From these observations, what did the doctors suggest to rich families to help their babies survive?

....

....

(1)

Continued on next page ▶

b) Sailors at that time often suffered from a disease called scurvy. Doctors thought that fresh fruit might help.

i) How could doctors test their idea on a ship's crew that was about to set off on a long journey?

....

....

....

....

....

(3)

ii) Complete the missing words in the sentences below.

The sailors were getting scurvy because they did not

have a b.................... diet.

When they ate limes, it provided the sailors

with ....

(2)

2 a) Write down **two** foods that help us to grow.

   ....
   (2)

   b) Write down **two** foods that contain large amounts of fat.

   ....
   (2)

   c) Which **one** of the foods below contains most sugar?

   Draw a ring around the correct food.

   JAM   cheese   carrot   meat
   (1)

   d) Marathon runners often eat a large meal the night before the race.

   Write down **one** food that would be good for them to include in their meal.

   ....
   (1)

   Explain why this would be useful for the marathon runner.

   Because ....

   ....
   (1)

3 A netball team was training to get fit.

Their coach had them running the length of the netball court in a relay race.

a) Write down **three** ways that training for 5 minutes would affect the girls.

1 ....

2 ....

3 ....
(3)

b) What job does the heart do in your body?

....
(1)

c) Which bones in your skeleton protect your heart? ....
(1)

d) Fill in the missing words in the sentences below.

The .... in the walls of your heart c.....................
regularly.

Your blood moves around your body in blood v..................... .
(3)

4 A group did a survey of the pulse rates of some other children in their class. They wanted to see if there was a difference between boys and girls.

Child	Resting pulse rate (beats per minute)			
	First try	Second try	Third try	Average (mean)
Neil (boy)	72	74	73	73
Sima (girl)	78	80	82	80
Liz (girl)	69	69	72	70
Tammy (girl)	81	79	77	79
Tim (boy)	65	65	65	65
Ben (boy)	82	82	79	81

a) Why are the pulse rates for each child taken three times?

....

....

....
(1)

Continued on next page

b) Use the grid below to draw a bar chart showing the average resting pulse rates.

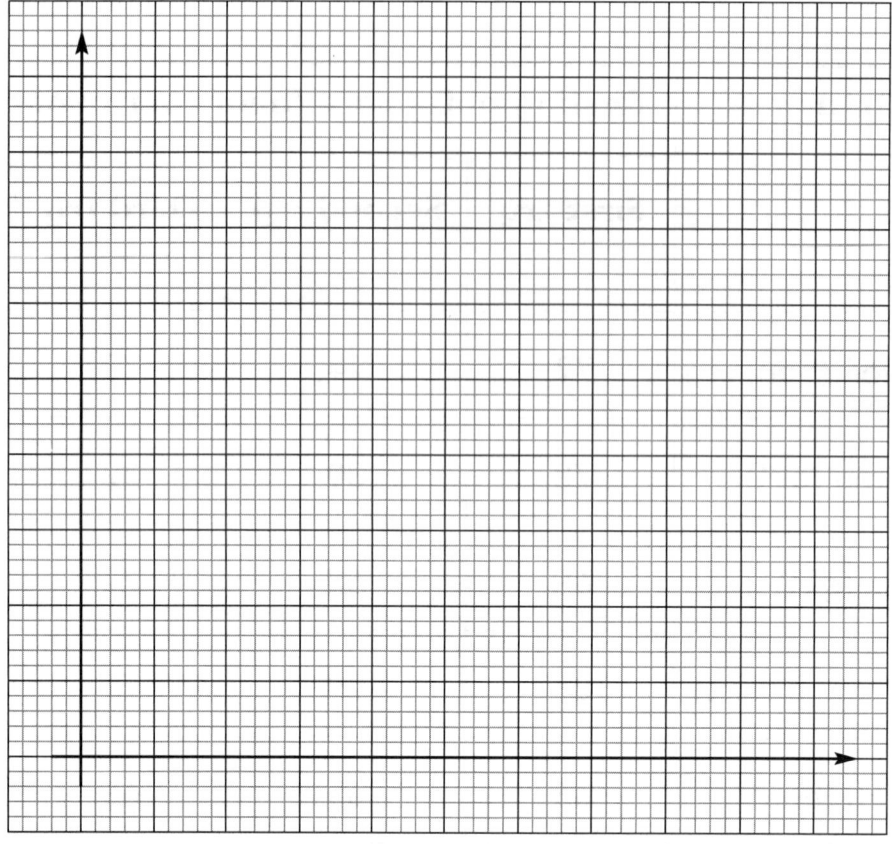

(8)

c) What do the results of this enquiry suggest? Is there any pattern?

....

....

....

(1)

5 A group of children wanted to test their idea that the longer you exercise, the higher your pulse rate goes.

They tested their prediction by taking Gemma's pulse after she had been running for different lengths of time.

Their results are in the table below.

Time running (minutes)	Pulse rate (beats per minute)
0	78
1	132
2	144
3	162
4	174

Use the grid on the next page to show these results on a line graph.

b) Do these results support the prediction made? ....

(1)

c) How could the group do this investigation, to be more certain of their results and conclusions?

....

(1)

d) Why does your heart beat faster when you exercise?

....

....

....

....

(2)

Continued on next page

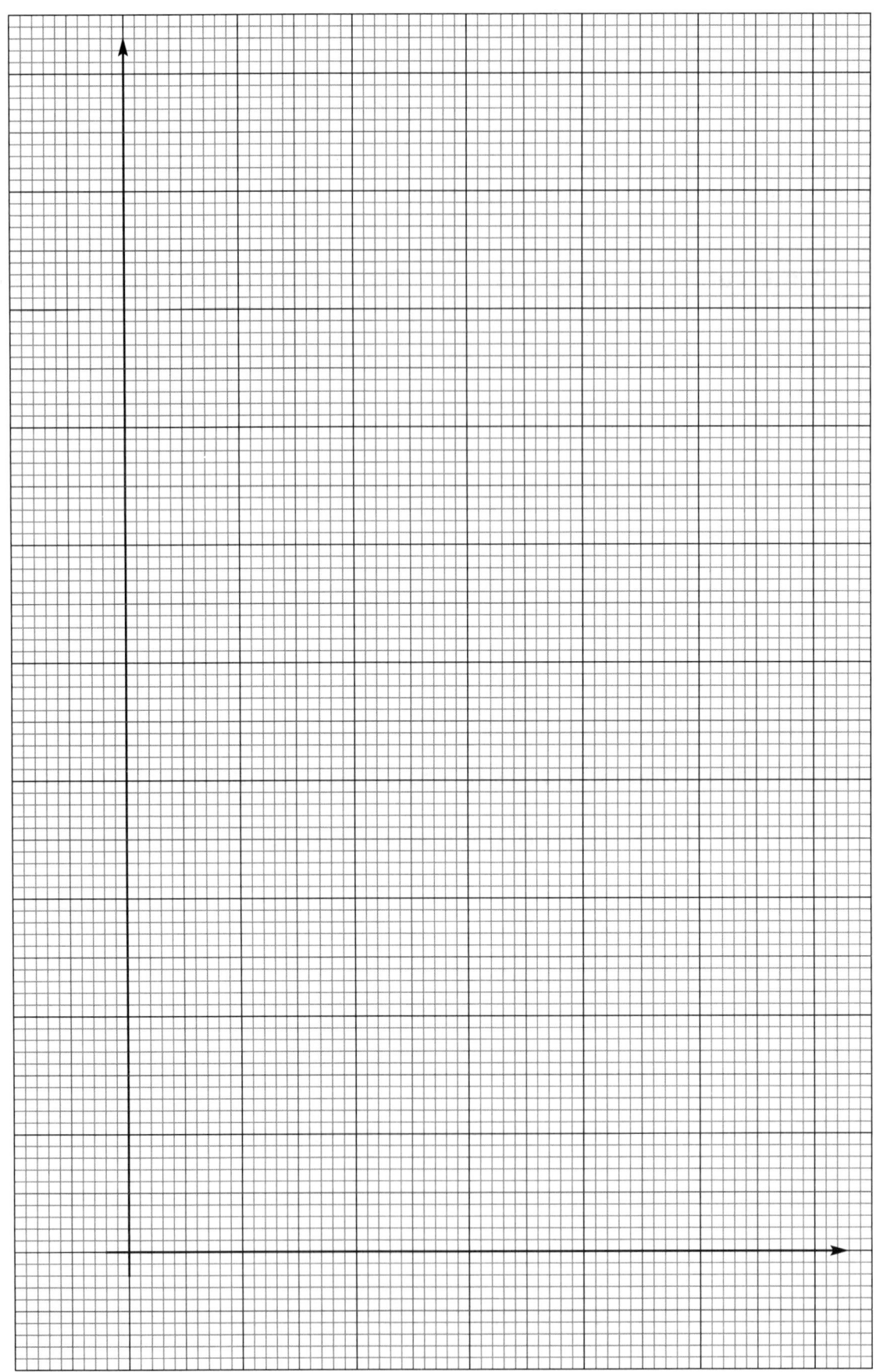

Grid for question 5

(10)

6 Alcohol and tobacco are types of drug.

a) What is a drug?

....

(1)

b) Name **one** part of the body that tobacco damages.

....

(1)

c) Name **one** part of the body that alcohol damages.

....

(1)

d) Write down **two** possible ways in which medicines may sometimes be harmful to a person.

1 ....

....

2 ....

....

(2)

KEEPING HEALTHY

Mark scheme

1	a)	Don't boil the milk/give fresh milk (breast feed).	1 mark
	b)	Give the crew fruit	1 mark
		but not to all crew	1 mark
		then see how many of each group got ill/scurvy.	1 mark
	c)	balanced	1 mark
		vitamins/vitamin C	1 mark
2	a)	any two protein rich foods	2 marks
	b)	any two fatty foods	2 marks
	c)	jam	1 mark
	d)	any starchy food e.g. pasta, rice	1 mark
	e)	Supplies source of energy.	1 mark
3	a)	Get hot.	1 mark
		Heart beats faster/higher pulse rate.	1 mark
		Breathe faster. (Allow 'Feel tired.')	1 mark
	b)	Pumps blood around the body.	1 mark
	c)	ribs	1 mark
	d)	muscle	1 mark
		contracts	1 mark
		vessels	1 mark
4	a)	To get more reliable results/to check results	1 mark
	b)	bar chart	
		1 mark for each correctly labelled axis	2 marks
		1 mark for each bar of correct height	6 marks
	c)	no pattern (or sensible alternative)	1 mark
5	a)	Vertical axis labelled 'Pulse rate'	1 mark
		Horizontal axis labelled 'Time'	1 mark
		Both sets of units included i.e. (beats per minute) and (minutes – allow 'mins')	1 mark
		Even scale used	1 mark
		1 mark for each point plotted correctly	5 marks
		Line drawn to join points	1 mark
	b)	yes	1 mark
	c)	Repeat readings/test more people.	1 mark
	d)	To increase blood/oxygen supply	1 mark
		to your muscles.	1 mark
6	a)	Something that affects the way your body works.	1 mark
	b)	lungs/heart	1 mark
	c)	liver/brain	1 mark
	d)	Don't follow instructions/take too much.	1 mark
		side effects/allergic reaction	1 mark

TOTAL: 50 marks

KEEPING HEALTHY

Recording teacher assessment using QCA Schemes of work

Class/year group: .... Teacher: ....

The majority of pupils have met the learning outcomes as stated in the medium-term plans from this QCA unit and they can:

- identify the components of a healthy and varied diet
- recognise some harmful effects of drugs
- recognise that during exercise the heart beats faster to take blood more rapidly to the muscles
- make careful measurements of pulse rates
- represent them in suitable graphs and explain what the graphs show.

+

Some have made more progress and can also:

- explain why they should make repeated measurements of pulse rate and why it is important to test the effects of exercise on the pulse rate of several people.

Names or initials
(Include explanatory notes as necessary.)

−

Some have not made this much progress but can:

- identify some foods needed for a healthy diet and some harmful effects of drugs
- recognise that pulse rate is a measure of how fast the heart is beating and make measurements of pulse rate.

Names or initials
(Include explanatory notes as necessary.)

The back of this sheet is on page 144.

KEEPING HEALTHY

My concept map

Name ....

Look at the words below. Link the boxes together and label the lines, explaining your links.

You might want to cut the boxes out and arrange them yourself on a clean piece of paper.

You could draw your own concept map, using the same words.

| heart |

| lungs | | blood |

| muscles | | healthy |

| ribs |

Complete the diagram

You will need coloured pens or pencils in **three** different colours for this task.

Follow these steps to complete the diagram below.

1. With your **first** colour, draw in the heart. Think about its shape and where it is in the chest.
2. Use your **second** colour to draw in the lungs.
3. Now use your **third** colour to draw in the ribs.

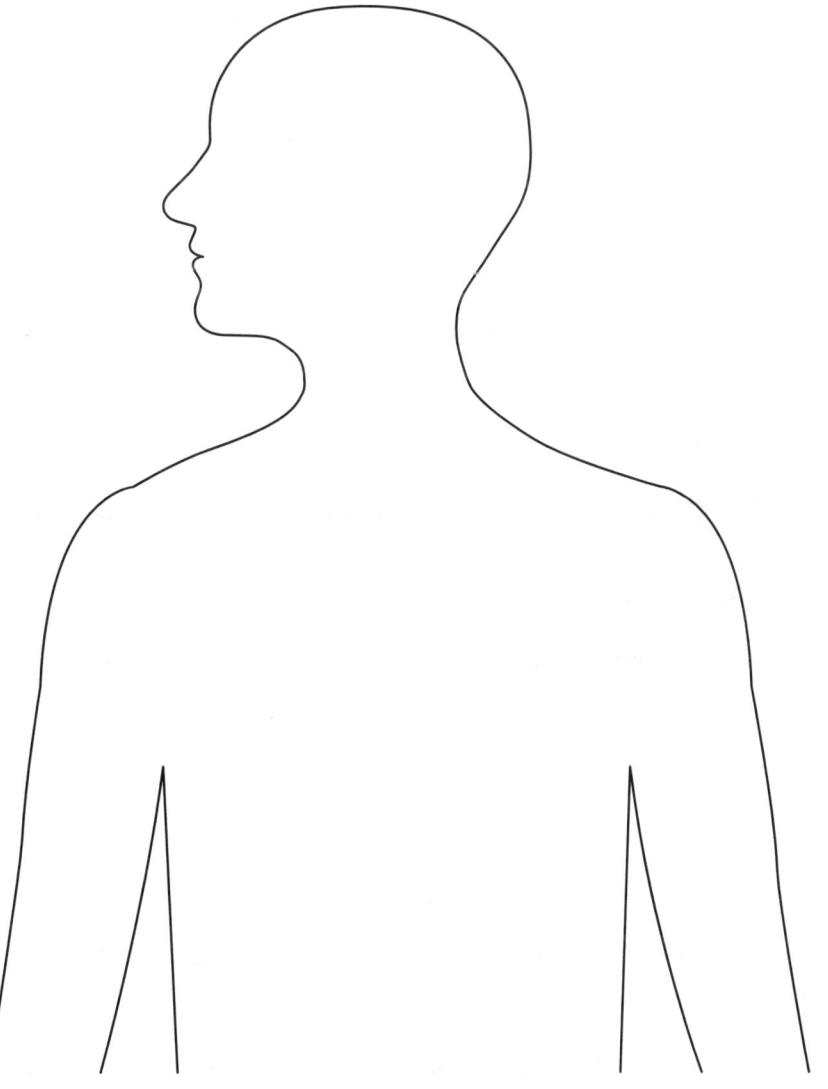

LIFE CYCLES

Pupil checklist

By the end of this unit:

I should know that:

- [ ] flowering plants reproduce
- [ ] seeds can be dispersed (spread out) in a number of ways
- [ ] many fruits and seeds are food for animals, including humans
- [ ] germination is the first growth of a seed
- [ ] seeds need water and warmth (but not light) to germinate
- [ ] insects pollinate some flowers
- [ ] plants produce flowers that have male and female organs
- [ ] seeds are formed when pollen (from the male organ) fertilises the ovum (in the female organ)
- [ ] adult animals have young that grow into adults which in turn produce young
- [ ] human young depend on adults for a relatively long time
- [ ] if living things did not reproduce they would eventually die out.

I should be able to:

- [ ] observe fruits and seeds carefully, compare them and draw some conclusions
- [ ] suggest conditions that might affect germination and plan how to test them
- [ ] carry out a fair test by changing just one factor at a time
- [ ] understand that I need to test several seeds to get reliable results in my experiments
- [ ] draw the life cycle of a plant, that includes pollination, fertilisation, seed production, seed dispersal and germination.

Assessment questions

Name .... **Class** .... **Date** ....

1 a) What do we mean by 'seed dispersal'?

....

....

(1)

b) Draw a line from each plant to the way its seeds are dispersed.

Seeds from ...   **Dispersed by ...**

burdock   wind

poppy   animals eating them

dandelion   explosion

strawberry   animals carrying them on their fur

(4)

2 a) Which of the seeds in the table below will germinate?

Write 'yes' or 'no' in the last column of the table.

Seeds	Conditions	Will the seed germinate?
A	very cold, no water, light	
B	very cold, no water, dark	
C	very cold, water, light	
D	very cold, water, dark	
E	warm, water, light	
F	warm, water, dark	
G	warm, no water, light	
H	warm, no water, dark	

(8)

b) Where would you do the test on seeds B?

....
(1)

c) How many seeds would you test in each set of conditions?
Explain your answer.

....

....
(2)

3 Look at the diagram of the inside of a flower, drawn below.

a) Choose words from this box to label the flower.

| sepal   ovary   stigma   stamen   petal   style |

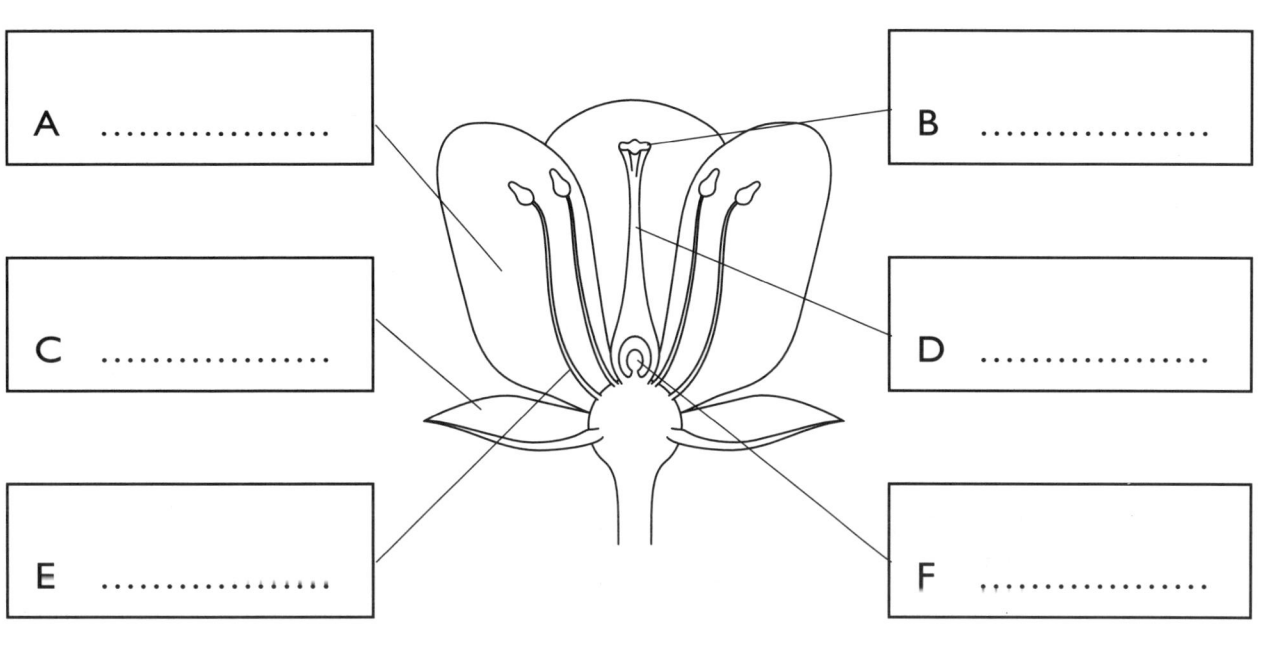

A ....

B ....

C ....

D ....

E ....

F ....

(6)

b) Choose words from part a) to complete the following sentences.

i) The .... makes pollen grains.

(1)

ii) The .... develops into a fruit.

(1)

iii) The .... attracts insects by its colour.

(1)

iv) Pollen grains from another plant stick to the ....

(1)

c) Write down **one** other way that pollen gets from one plant to another, apart from being carried by insects.

....

(1)

4 Look at the diagram of the life cycle of a flowering plant below.

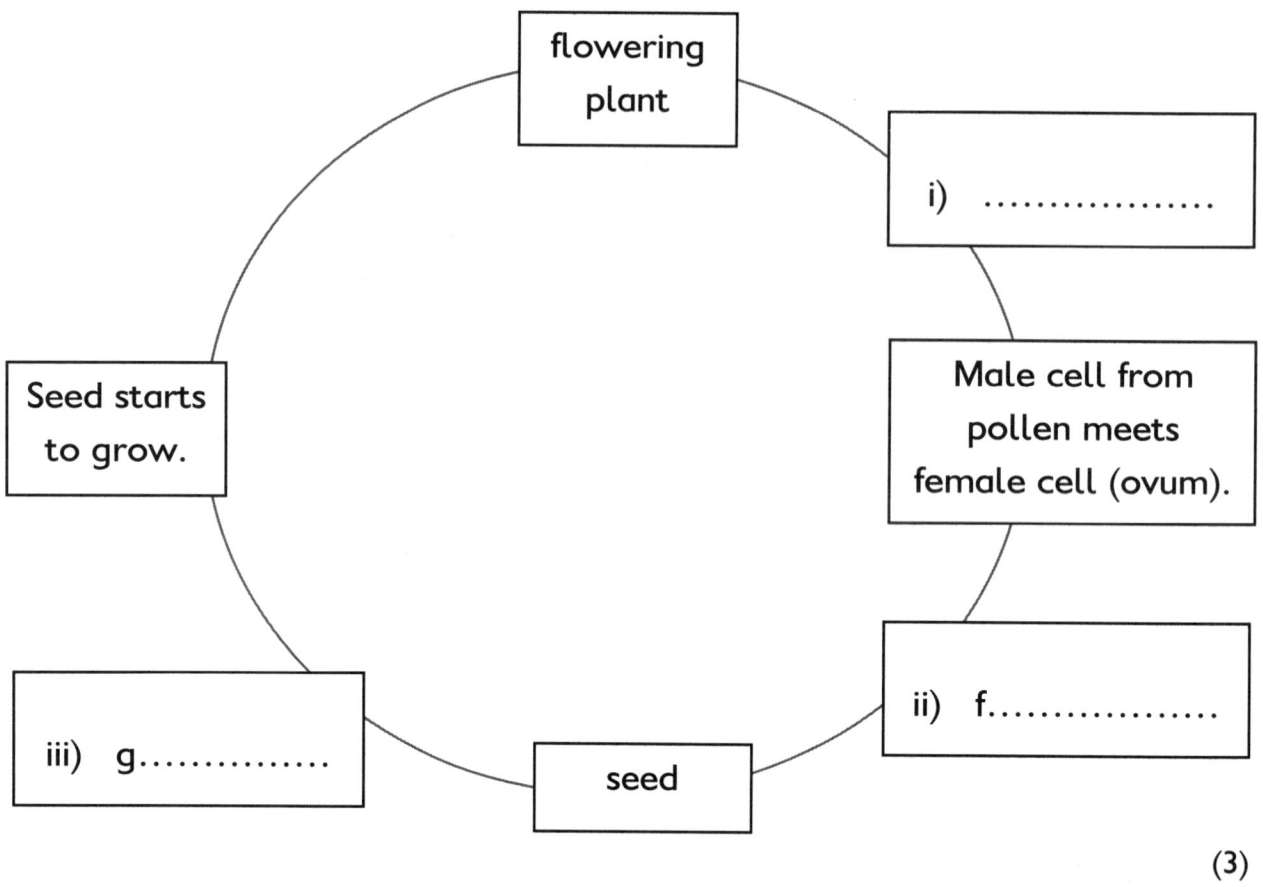

(3)

b) Where is the seed formed in a flowering plant?
Tick the box by the correct answer.

☐ In the stamen ☐ In the ovary

☐ In the style ☐ On the stigma

(1)

c) Why do plants produce lots of seeds?

....

(1)

d) Fill in the **two** missing words in the sentence below.

People who are allergic to pollen are said to suffer from

....

(1)

5 a) Put these stages in the human life cycle in order.

adolescence

babyhood

adulthood

childhood

First ....

Then ....

Then ....

Finally ....

(1)

b) The length of time between fertilisation and birth varies between animals.

Put these animals in order, according to the length of this time:

elephant, mouse, human.

Longest ....

Then ....

Shortest ....

(1)

c) The time between fertilisation and birth is called the

g......................... period.

(1)

LIFE CYCLES

Mark scheme

1	a)	seeds being spread out	1 mark
	b)	burdock → animals carrying them on their fur	1 mark
		poppy → explosion	1 mark
		dandelion → wind	1 mark
		strawberry → animal eating them	1 mark
2	a)	Seed A: no	1 mark
		Seed B: no	1 mark
		Seed C: no	1 mark
		Seed D: no	1 mark
		Seed E: yes	1 mark
		Seed F: yes	1 mark
		Seed G: no	1 mark
		Seed H: no	1 mark
	b)	in a 'fridge/freezer	1 mark
	c)	any number greater than or equal to 5	1 mark
		In order to get more reliable results/something might be wrong with the seed if you only tested one.	1 mark
3	a)	A) petal	1 mark
		B) stigma	1 mark
		C) sepal	1 mark
		D) style	1 mark
		E) stamen	1 mark
		F) ovary	1 mark
	b)	i) stamen	1 mark
		ii) ovary	1 mark
		iii) petal	1 mark
		iv) stigma	1 mark
	c)	by the wind	1 mark
4	a)	i) pollination	1 mark
		ii) fertilisation	1 mark
		iii) germination	1 mark
	b)	in the ovary	1 mark
	c)	Because not many go on to develop into new plants.	1 mark
	d)	hay fever	1 mark
5	a)	babyhood, childhood, adolescence, adulthood	1 mark
	b)	elephant, human, mouse	1 mark
	c)	gestation	1 mark

TOTAL: 36 marks

YEAR 5/6 UNIT 5B ASSESSMENT

LIFE CYCLES

Recording teacher assessment using QCA Schemes of work

Class/year group: .... Teacher: ....

The majority of pupils have met the learning outcomes as stated in the medium-term plans from this QCA unit and they can:

- name and explain the functions of some parts of a flower
- describe the processes of pollination, fertilisation, seed dispersal and germination
- explain how to carry out a fair test to find the conditions necessary for germination
- explain that living things need to reproduce if the species is to survive, and recognise stages in the growth of humans.

+
Some have made more progress and can also:

- explain why it is important to use a number of seeds or plants in an investigation into growth or germination.

Names or initials
(Include explanatory notes as necessary.)

–
Some have not made this much progress but can:

- name the parts of a flower and explain how pollen and seeds are dispersed
- describe some of the conditions tested in investigating germination and recognise some stages in the development of humans.

Names or initials
(Include explanatory notes as necessary.)

The back of this sheet is on page 144.

LIFE CYCLES

My concept map

Name ....

Look at the words below. Link the boxes together and label the lines, explaining your links.

You might want to cut the boxes out and arrange them yourself on a clean piece of paper.

You could draw your own concept map, using the same words.

seeds

fertilisation   **germination**

pollination   **dispersal**

flower

Anagrams

LIFE CYCLES

Solve the anagrams below to find the key words in this unit.

1   This is the process in which pollen gets from one plant to another.

    l P l i t n o o a n i

    The word is __ __ __ __ __ __ __ __ __ __ __ .

2   This is the process in which the male cell from pollen joins with the ovum.

    e r i F i s i t o t n l a

    The word is __ __ __ __ __ __ __ __ __ __ __ __ __ .

3   This is the process in which a seed forms a shoot and starts growing.

    m e n i t G i n a o r

    The word is __ __ __ __ __ __ __ __ __ __ __ .

GASES AROUND US

Pupil checklist

By the end of this unit:

I should know that:

- [ ] air has weight and is all around us
- [ ] powders and sponges are solids that have air in their gaps
- [ ] my observations and measurements may need to be repeated
- [ ] soils have air trapped within them
- [ ] there are many gases and many of these are important to us
- [ ] gases are formed when liquids evaporate
- [ ] gases flow and spread out more easily than liquids
- [ ] you can easily change the volume of a gas but not the volume of a liquid or solid.

I should be able to:

- [ ] recognise differences between solids and liquids
- [ ] explain some effects of air in everyday life and in experiments
- [ ] observe materials carefully and explain what I see
- [ ] measure volumes of water carefully
- [ ] use my results to compare the air trapped in different soils
- [ ] explain observations when water evaporates in different places
- [ ] describe differences in properties between solids, liquids and gases.

Science Assessment Y5/6   © Lawrie Ryan, Nelson Thornes Ltd. 2002

GASES AROUND US

Assessment questions

Name .... Class .... Date ....

1 a) Here are some properties of solids, liquids and gases.

Next to each property, write down whether it describes a solid, a liquid or a gas. Some properties may have more than one answer.

Property	Solid, liquid or gas
Keeps its own shape.	
Takes the shape of its container.	
Can be squashed quite easily.	
Is very difficult to squash.	
Can flow.	

(8)

b) Explain what is happening in this experiment.

....

....

(2)

Science Assessment Y5/6   © Lawrie Ryan, Nelson Thornes Ltd. 2002

2 a) We can think of sponge and lemonade as mixtures.

Draw lines between the materials and the words 'solid', 'liquid' or 'gas'.
Each of the materials will have more than one line.

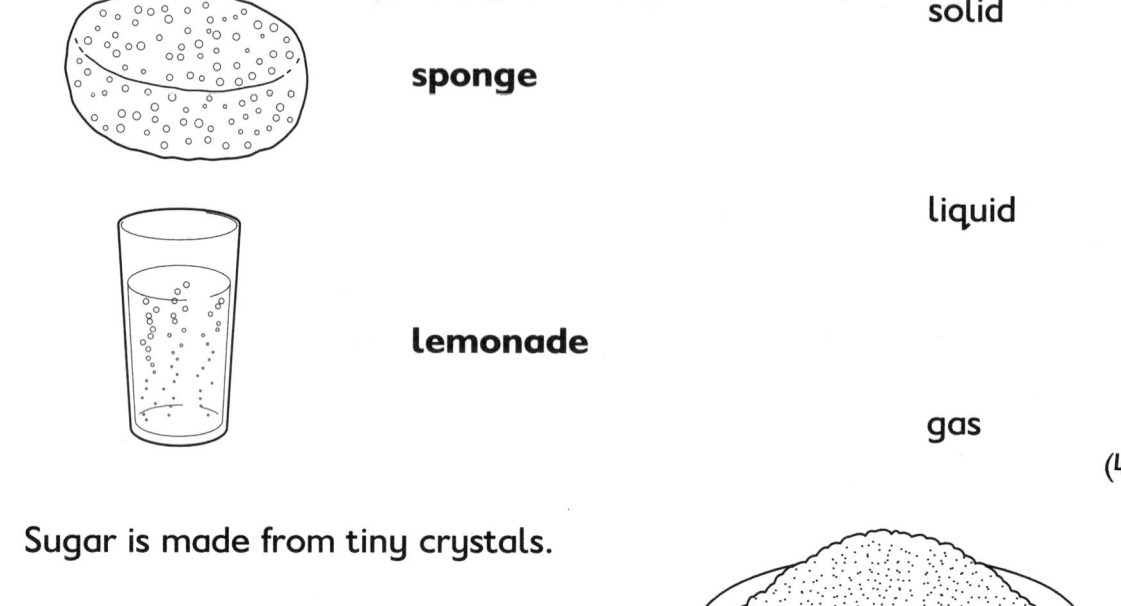

solid

sponge

liquid

lemonade

gas

(4)

b) Sugar is made from tiny crystals.

What is in the gaps between the crystals of sugar?

....

(1)

3 Read the volume of water shown in each tube below.

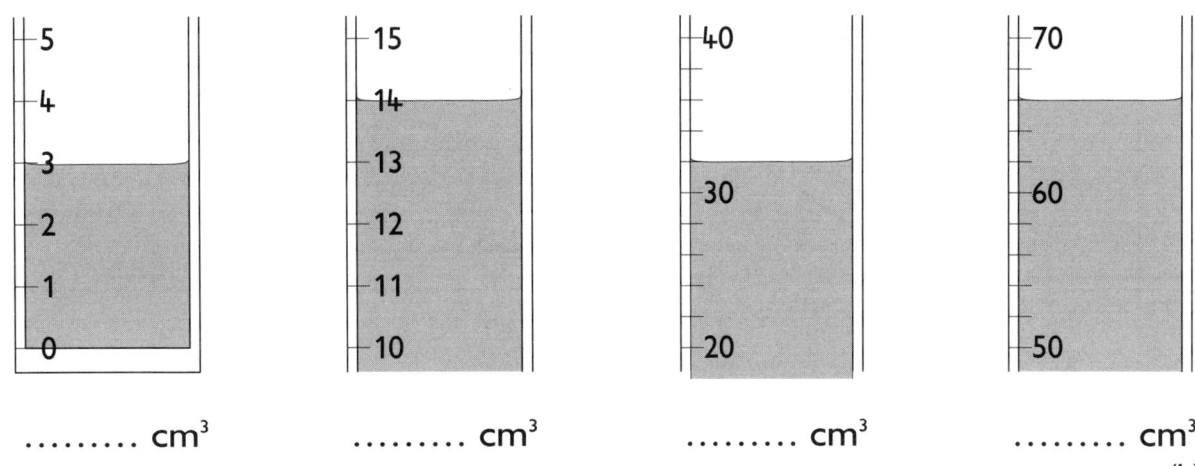

.... cm³   .... cm³   .... cm³   .... cm³

(4)

b) A group of children were looking at three different types of soil. They labelled them A, B and C.

One test they did was to pour water on the soils.
They added the water from a measuring cylinder until some stayed on top of the soil. They used the same volume of soil in each test.

Look at their table of results, shown below.

	Soil A	Soil B	Soil C
Volume of water to start with in the measuring cylinder (cm³)	100	100	100
Volume of water left in the measuring cylinder (cm³)	60	55	72

Use the results in the table to work out how much water was absorbed by each soil.

Soil A: .... cm³   Soil B: .... cm³   Soil C: .... cm³

(3)

c) Give **one** reason why some soils absorb more water than others.

....

(1)

4   a) Which of the following are normally gases?

   Draw a ring around the name of each gas.

   ```
   helium
              carbon
                            oxygen
   diesel

          carbon dioxide
                            petrol

       milk           nitrogen
   ```

   (4)

   b) Which gas from the box above do we use when we breathe?

   ....
   (1)

   c) Which gas from the box above do we sometimes use to fill balloons so they will float in the air?

   ....
   (1)

   d) Which gas from the box above puts the 'fizz' in cola and lemonade?

   ....
   (1)

   e) Which gas from the box above makes up most of the air around us?

   ....
   (1)

5 Amy and her family went to France for their holidays.

Amy left a glass of water on her bedroom windowsill at home.

When she returned from holiday, the glass was empty.

a) What had happened to the water?

   ....
   (1)

b) Amy bought a bottle of perfume as a present for her friend.

   The bottle was in a plastic bag, but as soon as her case was opened she knew it had broken.
   How did she know?

   ....
   (1)

c) Amy's dad could smell gas when he went into the kitchen.

   Why was he worried in case there was a gas leak?

   ....
   (1)

d) What is the name of the gas we use in gas cookers?

   Draw a ring around the correct answer.

   artificial gas   natural gas   fire gas   flame gas
   (1)

e) The gas in part c) does not smell, so how did Amy's dad know there might be a gas leak?

   ....

   ....
   (1)

6 a) Why can you smell paint all around a house when a room has been decorated?

....

....
(2)

b) You are given a jar with a coloured gas inside it and another jar full of a liquid.

If you turn each jar on its side and remove the lid, what would you see?

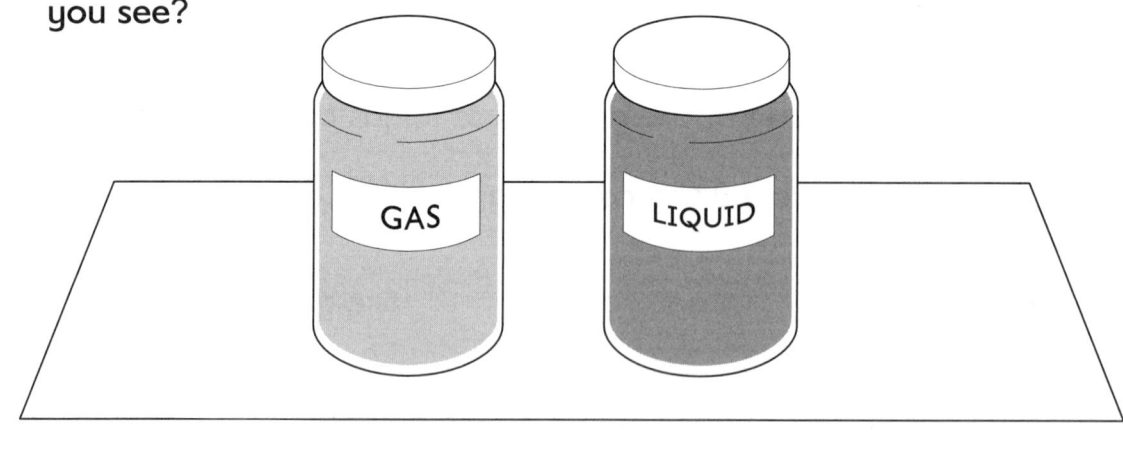

....

....
(2)

GASES AROUND US

Mark scheme

1. a)

Property	Solid, liquid or gas
Keeps its own shape.	solid (1)
Takes the shape of its container.	liquid (1), gas (1)
Can be squashed quite easily.	gas (1)
Is very difficult to squash.	solid (1), liquid (1)
Can flow.	liquid (1), gas (1)

8 marks

b) The balloon filled with air in is heavier — 1 mark
because air
has mass/does weigh something. (Give both marks if this is given.) — 1 mark

2. a) sponge → solid — 1 mark
sponge → gas — 1 mark
lemonade → liquid — 1 mark
lemonade → gas — 1 mark

b) air — 1 mark

3. a) 3 — 1 mark
14 — 1 mark
32 — 1 mark
66 — 1 mark

b) 40 — 1 mark
45 — 1 mark
20 — 1 mark

c) There are more gaps between particles/More air is trapped in it. — 1 mark

4. a) helium — 1 mark
oxygen — 1 mark
carbon dioxide — 1 mark
nitrogen   (Take 1 mark off for each extra alternative ringed.) — 1 mark

b) oxygen — 1 mark

c) helium — 1 mark

d) carbon dioxide — 1 mark

e) nitrogen

5. a) It had evaporated. (Allow 'Gone into the air.') — 1 mark

b) She could smell it. — 1 mark

c) danger of explosion/fire — 1 mark

d) natural gas — 1 mark

e) Another gas that does smell is added to it. — 1 mark

6. a) Liquid from paint evaporates — 1 mark
then spreads/flows all around the house. — 1 mark

b) Gas spreads out in all directions. — 1 mark
Liquid pours out/flows/spreads out on table. — 1 mark

TOTAL: 40 marks

GASES AROUND US

Recording teacher assessment using QCA Schemes of work

Class/year group: …………………… Teacher: ……………………………………

The majority of pupils have met the learning outcomes as stated in the medium-term plans from this QCA unit and they can:

- recognise that air is a material and that it is one of a range of gases that have important uses
- recognise that liquids evaporate to form gases and that gases change shape and flow from place to place
- measure volumes of liquids accurately, recognise when observations and measurements need to be repeated and provide explanations for what they observe in term of knowledge and understanding about gases.

+

Some have made more progress and can also:

- explain the relationships between liquids and solids in terms of evaporation, make clear distinctions between the properties of solids, liquids and gases and explain why observations need to be repeated.

Names or initials
(Include explanatory notes as necessary.)

−

Some have not made this much progress but can:

- state that air is a gas
- recognise that gases flow from place, and measure volumes of liquid.

Names or initials
(Include explanatory notes as necessary.)

The back of this sheet is on page 144.

YEAR 5/6 UNIT 5C ASSESSMENT

GASES AROUND US

My concept map

Name ....

Look at the words below. Link the boxes together and label the lines, explaining your links.

You might want to cut the boxes out and arrange them yourself on a clean piece of paper.

You could draw your own concept map, using the same words.

gas

liquid   solid

helium   water

GASES AROUND US

Complete the diagram

Draw labelled arrows on the diagram below to show what happens when you take the top off a bottle of perfume.

CHANGING STATE

Pupil checklist

By the end of this unit:

I should know that:

- [ ] evaporation is when a liquid turns to a gas
- [ ] water is *not* the only liquid that evaporates
- [ ] condensation is when a gas turns to a liquid
- [ ] condensation is the reverse of evaporation
- [ ] air contains water vapour which condenses on cold surfaces
- [ ] the boiling point (boiling temperature) of water is 100°C
- [ ] changes of state (melting, freezing, condensing, evaporating) are reversible changes
- [ ] water evaporates from seas or lakes, then condenses as clouds and eventually falls as rain
- [ ] water collects in streams and rivers and flows back to the sea.

I should be able to:

- [ ] use the word 'evaporation' when explaining observations (such as washing drying) and results from investigations
- [ ] test ideas and make predictions
- [ ] decide what evidence to collect and plan, then carry out, a fair test
- [ ] make careful measurements and record them in tables and graphs
- [ ] spot patterns in results and use them to draw conclusions
- [ ] use patterns in results to make further predictions, and to decide if evidence collected supports the prediction
- [ ] use my knowledge of changes of state to explain the water cycle.

CHANGING STATE

Assessment questions

Name .... Class .... Date ....

1 a) Simon had been playing football all lunchtime and was hot and sweaty when he came back into class.

After he leaned on his table, he noticed a damp hand print was left there.

a) What did Simon see as he watched his hand print for a few minutes?

....

....
(2)

b) Explain Simon's observations in part a).

....

....
(1)

c) Simon's mum washed his shirt as soon as he got home. She was going to hang it out to dry on a washing line. What would be the best weather conditions to help the shirt dry quickly?

....
(2)

d) Simon wanted to help and asked if he could peg the shirt on the line.   A   B   C

Which way, A, B or C, should Simon hang the shirt? ....
(1)

Science Assessment Y5/6   © Lawrie Ryan, Nelson Thornes Ltd. 2002

42

2 Children in a class were investigating the factors that might affect how quickly water evaporates.

One group decided to look at temperature.

They put one glass of water in the classroom and one in a cold shed outside.

They measured the water level every two days.

a) Write down **two** things the group needed to keep the same, to make it a fair test.

1 ....

2 ....

(2)

b) The group's results are shown in the table below.

Time (days)	Height of water in classroom (mm)	Height of water in shed (mm)
0	65	65
2	61	64
4	57	62
6	53	62
8	47	60
10	44	58

Continued on next page

Science Assessment Y5/6   © Lawrie Ryan, Nelson Thornes Ltd. 2002

Draw two lines to show their results, on the graph below.

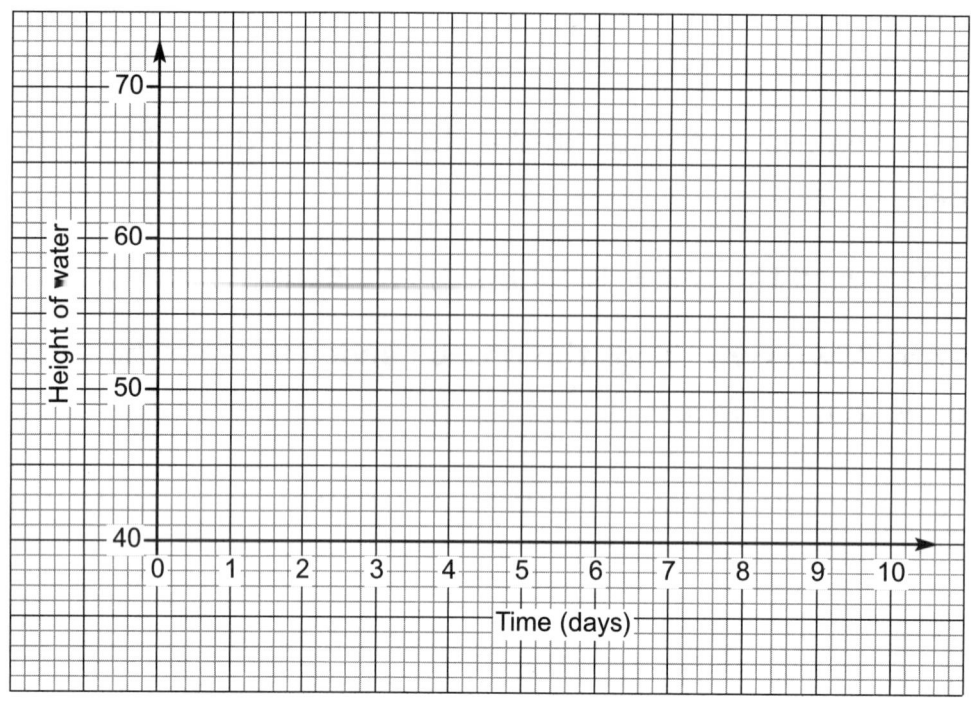

(6)

c) Where did the water evaporate more quickly, in the classroom or the shed?

....

(1)

d) What do you think caused the difference between the two sets of results?

....

(1)

e) What pattern would you expect if you did more experiments to test out your idea from part d)?

....

....

(2)

3 Look at the drawing of the experiment below.

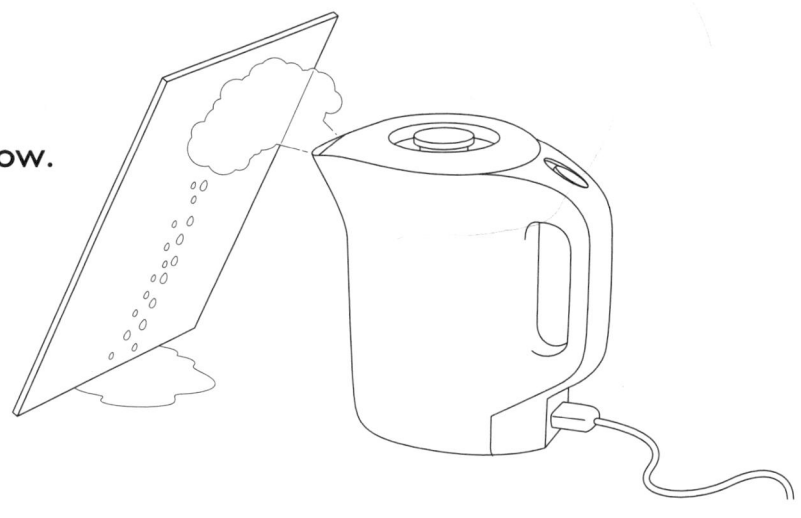

a) Describe and explain your observations about the experiment.

....

....

....
(2)

b) Sometimes the windows in a kitchen mist up.

A

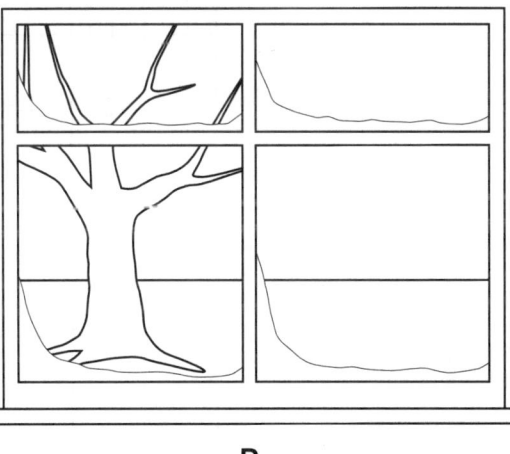

B

Which window, A or B, is more likely to mist up in the kitchen?

....
(1)

c) Explain your answer to part b).

....

....
(2)

4 A temperature sensor was used to monitor the temperature of some water as it was heated in a pan.

Here is the graph to show what happened in the first three minutes.

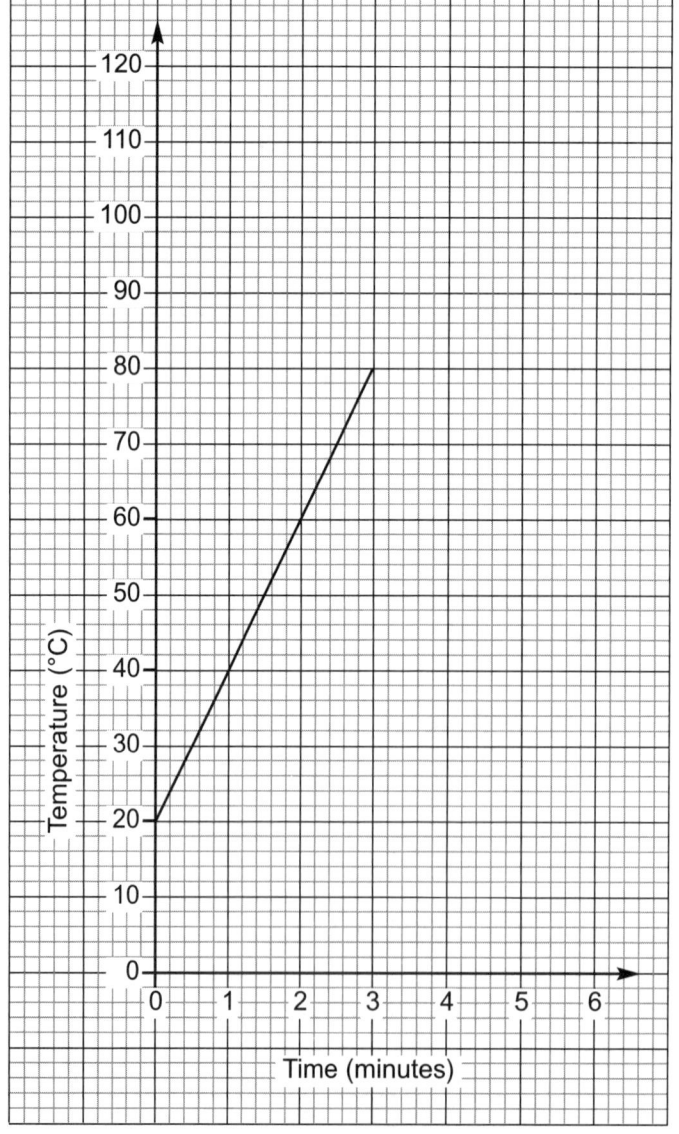

Use the graph to answer the following questions.

Continued on next page

a) By how much did the temperature of the water rise each minute?

.... °C

(1)

b) Continue the line on the graph above to show what happens if you heat the water for 5 minutes.

(2)

c) What was room temperature that day? .... °C

(2)

d) Suppose you do the same experiment again, but this time the cooker is turned higher.
Draw the line you would expect on the graph.

(2)

5 Look at the diagram below.

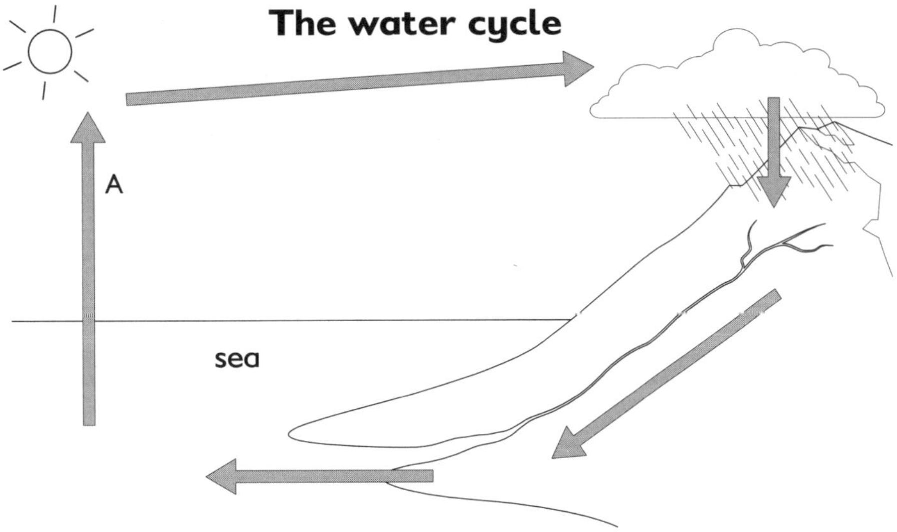

The water cycle

A

sea

a) What is the name of the process labelled A? ....

(1)

b) How does water from the hills get back to the sea?

....

(1)

c) Describe how clouds are formed.

....

....

(2)

CHANGING STATE

Mark scheme

1	a)	The hand print gets smaller	1 mark
		then disappears.	1 mark
	b)	water/sweat evaporated	1 mark
	c)	hot (warm)/dry/windy (any two)	2 marks
	d)	C	1 mark
2	a)	same amount/volume of water	1 mark
		same size/shape glasses	1 mark
	b)	3 marks for each set of data plotted correctly and joined with lines	6 marks
	c)	classroom	1 mark
	d)	Different temperatures/colder in shed/hotter in classroom.	1 mark
	e)	The higher the temperature/hotter it is, the more quickly the water evaporates.	2 marks
		(1 mark only for specific case, e.g. 'The hot water evaporates more quickly.')	
3	a)	Water vapour is cooled down by cold mirror	1 mark
		and then condenses back into water.	1 mark
	b)	B	1 mark
	c)	The glass is colder in B	1 mark
		so the water vapour condenses (more quickly).	1 mark
4	a)	20	1 mark
	b)	Line carries on upwards in straight line.	1 mark
		Line levels off at 100°C at 4 minutes.	1 mark
	c)	20 (1) °C (1)	2 marks
	d)	Steeper line rising from origin.	1 mark
		Line levels off at 100°C before 4 minutes.	1 mark
5	a)	evaporation	1 mark
	b)	rivers/streams	1 mark
	c)	Water vapour cools down	1 mark
		and condenses.	1 mark

TOTAL: 34 marks

YEAR 5/6 — UNIT 5D ASSESSMENT

CHANGING STATE

Recording teacher assessment using QCA Schemes of work

Class/year group: .... Teacher: ....

The majority of pupils have met the learning outcomes as stated in the medium-term plans from this QCA unit and they can:

- name and describe examples of the main processes associated with water changing state and recognise that these processes can be reversed
- explain the water cycle in terms of these processes
- use patterns in data to make predictions.

+

Some have made more progress and can also:

- explain how changing conditions affects processes such as evaporation and condensation, and use patterns in data to give reasons for predictions made.

Names or initials
(Include explanatory notes as necessary.)

−

Some have not made this much progress but can:

- describe how to change water into ice and steam, and steam into water
- describe a few examples where these changes occur, and recognise patterns in data.

Names or initials
(Include explanatory notes as necessary.)

The back of this sheet is on page 144.

Science Assessment Y5/6   © Lawrie Ryan, Nelson Thornes Ltd. 2002

CHANGING STATE

My concept map

Name ....

Look at the words below. Link the boxes together and label the lines, explaining your links.

You might want to cut the boxes out and arrange them yourself on a clean piece of paper.

You could draw your own concept map, using the same words.

| solid |

| liquid | | gas |

| clouds | | sea |

| water |

EARTH, SUN AND MOON

Pupil checklist

By the end of this unit:

I should know that:

- [ ] the Earth, Sun and Moon are roughly spherical (shaped like a ball)
- [ ] the Sun is larger than the Earth, and the Earth is larger than the Moon
- [ ] the Sun appears to move across the sky as the day passes
- [ ] evidence can be interpreted in more than one way
- [ ] the Earth moves around (orbits) the Sun, and the Moon moves around the Earth
- [ ] the Earth spins on its own axis, once every 24 hours
- [ ] the Sun rises in the east and sets in the west
- [ ] it takes the Earth a year to orbit the Sun, spinning as it goes
- [ ] it takes the Moon about 28 days to orbit the Earth
- [ ] observations of the Moon give us evidence for a 28 day cycle.

I should be able to:

- [ ] collect information about the Earth, Sun and Moon to test ideas
- [ ] explain night and day
- [ ] make observations about where the Sun rises and sets, and to spot patterns in the data
- [ ] draw a graph of sunrise and sunset, and to spot patterns in the data.

Science Assessment Y5/6   © Lawrie Ryan, Nelson Thornes Ltd. 2002

YEAR 5/6 UNIT 5E ASSESSMENT

EARTH, SUN AND MOON

Assessment questions

Name .... Class .... Date ....

1 a) Which of these best describes the shape of the Moon? Tick the box.

☐ crescent ☐ circle ☐ sphere ☐ semi-circle

(1)

b) How could you use a ship to gain evidence that the Earth is not flat?

....

(1)

c) Put the Earth, Sun and Moon in order of size.

Largest .... Then .... Smallest ....

(1)

2 a) Which of these statements are true? Tick the boxes.

☐ The Earth orbits the Sun. ☐ The Earth orbits the Moon.
☐ The Sun orbits the Earth. ☐ The Moon orbits the Earth.
☐ The Earth spins like this. ☐ The Earth spins like this.

☐ It takes the Earth 24 hours to spin around once.
☐ It takes the Earth 28 days to spin around once.
☐ It takes the Earth 1 year to spin around once.

(4)

b) Explain how we get night and day on Earth.

....

....

(2)

Science Assessment Y5/6   © Lawrie Ryan, Nelson Thornes Ltd. 2002

3 a) Draw a line on the picture below to show the path of the Sun across the sky.

Put arrows on your line to show which way the Sun appears to move.

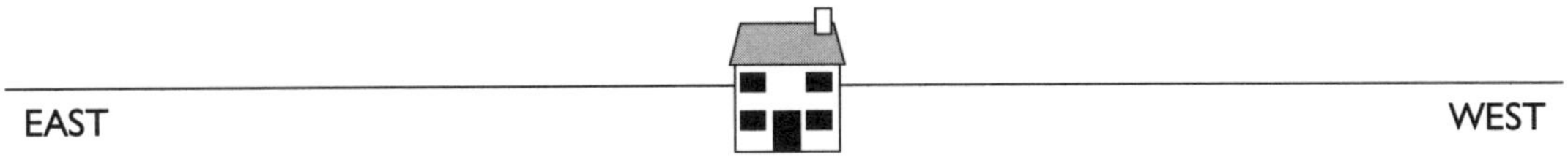

EAST   WEST

(2)

b) Draw a cross (✘) to show when the shadow of the house will be shortest.

(1)

c) Why does the Sun appear to move across the sky?

....

(1)

d) Which of these statements are true?

Tick the boxes by the correct answers.

☐ The Sun rises earlier in winter than in summer.

☐ The Sun rises earlier in summer than in winter.

☐ The Sun rises at the same time all year round.

☐ The Sun sets earlier in winter than in summer.

☐ The Sun sets earlier in summer than in winter.

☐ The Sun sets at the same time all year round.

(2)

4 The diagram below is not drawn to scale.

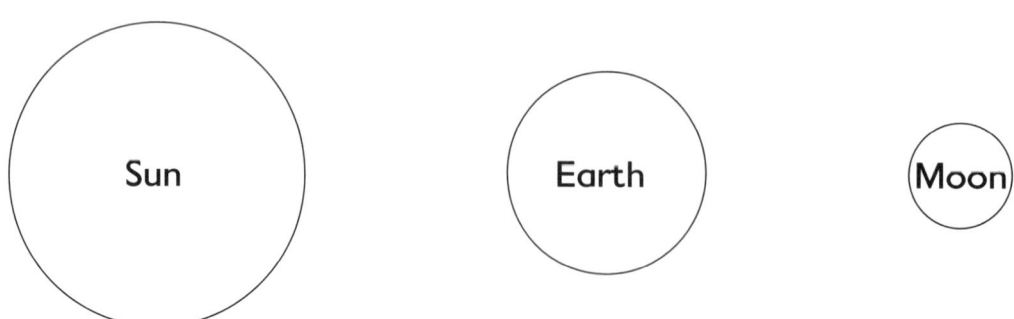

a) Draw two rings on the diagram above to show how the Sun and Earth, and the Earth and Moon move around each other.

(2)

b) On each line you have drawn, write down how long it takes for one complete orbit.

(2)

c) Which of these statements is true?

Tick the box by the correct answer.

☐ We can see the whole surface of the Moon during its cycle.

☐ We can only see one side of the Moon during its cycle.

(1)

EARTH, SUN AND MOON

Mark scheme

1 a) sphere — 1 mark

b) Sail in one general direction and arrive back where you started / sail ship away and watch it disappear over the horizon. — 1 mark

c) Largest – the Sun
then – the Earth
smallest – the Moon — 1 mark

2 a) The Earth orbits the Sun. — 1 mark
The Moon orbits the Earth. — 1 mark
The Earth spins like this:

— 1 mark

It takes the Earth 24 hours to spin around once. — 1 mark

b) As the Earth spins — 1 mark
it is daytime on the side facing Sun/night facing away. — 1 mark

3 a) Line arching across sky. — 1 mark
Arrows indicate Sun moving from east to west. — 1 mark

b) ✗ directly above house on line drawn — 1 mark

c) The Earth spins. — 1 mark

d) The Sun rises earlier in summer than in winter. — 1 mark
The Sun sets earlier in winter than in summer. — 1 mark

4 a) Line showing Earth going around Sun. — 1 mark
Line showing Moon going around Earth. — 1 mark

b) 1 year or 365 days (and a quarter) on line showing Earth going around Sun. — 1 mark
28 days (allow one month) on line showing Moon going around Earth. — 1 mark

c) We can only see one side of the Moon during its cycle. — 1 mark

TOTAL: 20 marks

EARTH, SUN AND MOON

Recording teacher assessment using QCA Schemes of work

Class/year group: .... Teacher: ....

The majority of pupils have met the learning outcomes as stated in the medium-term plans from this QCA unit and they can:

- recognise that the Earth, Sun and Moon are spherical, and support this with some evidence
- explain in terms of the rotation of the Earth why shadows change and the Sun appears to move across the sky during the course of the day
- recognise that it is daylight in the part of the Earth facing the Sun, that the Moon orbits the Earth and identify patterns in secondary data about sunrise and sunset.

+

Some have made more progress and can also:

- explain that the changes in the appearance of the Moon over a period of 28 days arise from the Moon orbiting the Earth once every 28 days (approximately)
- independently represent times of sunrise and sunset in graphs.

Names or initials
(Include explanatory notes as necessary.)

−

Some have not made this much progress but can:

- recognise that the Earth, Sun and Moon are spherical, and describe how shadows change as the Sun appears to move across the sky.

Names or initials
(Include explanatory notes as necessary.)

The back of this sheet is on page 144.

Science Assessment Y5/6   © Lawrie Ryan, Nelson Thornes Ltd. 2002

YEAR 5/6 UNIT 5E ASSESSMENT

EARTH, SUN AND MOON

My concept map

Name ....

Look at the words below. Link the boxes together and label the lines, explaining your links.

You might want to cut the boxes out and arrange them yourself on a clean piece of paper.

You could draw your own concept map, using the same words.

| Sun |

| Earth | | Moon |

| 24 hours | | year |

| 28 days |

YEAR 5/6 UNIT 5E ASSESSMENT

EARTH, SUN AND MOON

Ideas about our solar system

In your group, look at the children's ideas in the cartoon below.

Discuss their ideas.

Which do you agree with?

Carry out some research to see who is right.

- I think the Sun goes round the Earth.
- I think that the Moon grows and shrinks as it goes around the Earth.
- I think the Sun is the centre of our Solar System and the Earth and other planets go round it.
- I think that the Earth takes a year to spin round once on its own axis.

CHANGING SOUNDS

Pupil checklist

By the end of this unit:

I should know that:

- [ ] sounds are made by objects vibrating
- [ ] vibrations from sources of sound travel through different materials to my ear
- [ ] some materials are good at stopping vibrations from sound sources reaching my ear
- [ ] the word 'pitch' describes how high or low a sound is
- [ ] the pitch of a drum depends on its size and tightness of its skin
- [ ] high and low sounds can be loud or soft
- [ ] the pitch of a stringed instrument depends on the length, thickness and tightness of the string
- [ ] wind instruments make sounds because air vibrates.

I should be able to:

- [ ] make careful observations
- [ ] draw conclusions about sounds from my observations
- [ ] make predictions about which materials are effective at muffling sound
- [ ] plan a fair test to see how well different materials muffle sound
- [ ] carry out the fair test I planned
- [ ] use my results to check my prediction, and judge if my results are good enough to trust
- [ ] suggest how to change the pitch and loudness of a drum, stringed or wind instrument, and to test my ideas out
- [ ] listen carefully to sounds made, and record these in a table
- [ ] describe how the pitch of a wind instrument depends on the length of the vibrating air column
- [ ] use what I have learned about sound to explain how a range of musical instruments work.

CHANGING SOUNDS

Assessment questions

Name .... Class .... Date ....

1 a) Look at the picture below.

Anna whispers a message to Tom.

Explain how the message gets to Tom.

....

....
(2)

b) Anna talks more loudly at her end of the 'phone'.

What is the difference in the string now?

....
(1)

c) If the string is loose, the 'phone' does not work. Why not?

....
(1)

2 a) You can make a sound by blowing across the top of a bottle.

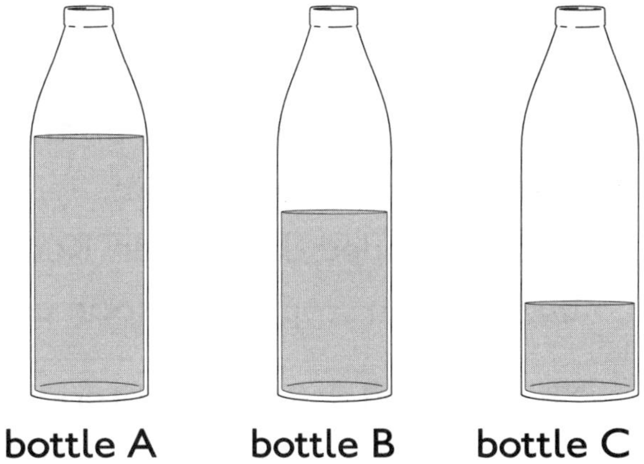

bottle A   bottle B   bottle C

Which bottle, A, B or C, will give the sound with the highest pitch?

.... (1)

b) What vibrates in the bottle to make the sound? .... (1)

c) Three identical elastic bands were plucked.

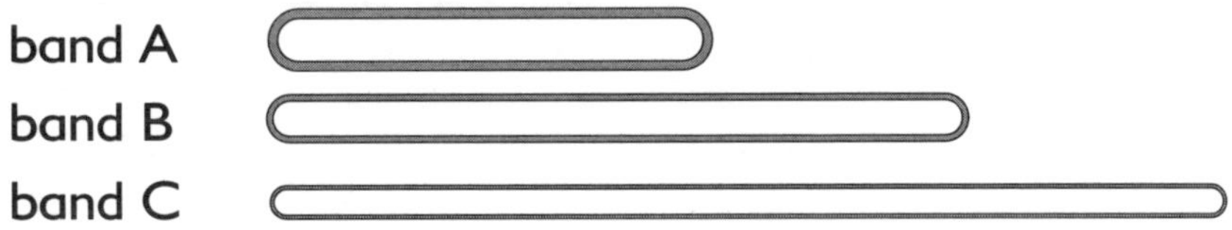

band A
band B
band C

i) Which band, A, B or C, made the sound with the lowest pitch?

.... (1)

ii) What could you do to make the bands make a louder sound?

.... (1)

d) These rulers were strummed.

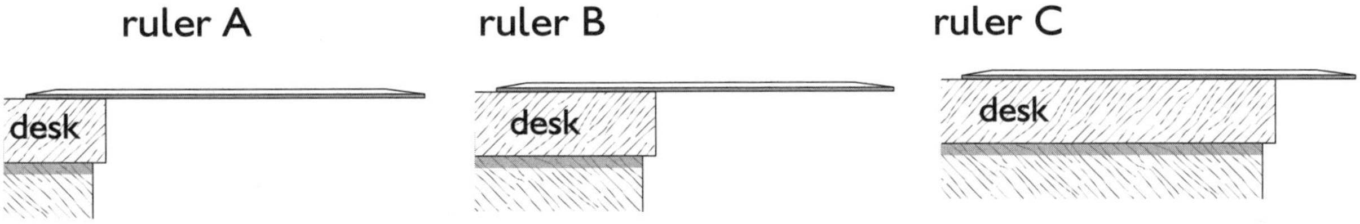

ruler A   ruler B   ruler C

Which ruler, A, B or C makes the sound with the highest pitch?

.... (1)

3 Katrina and Robin wanted to see which material was best at muffling sound. They set up the test shown in the diagram.

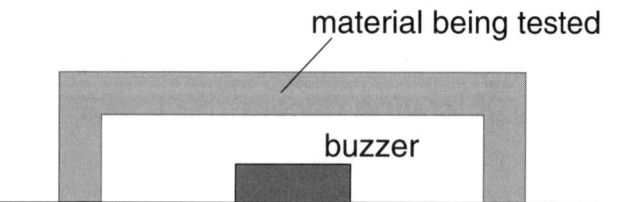

Robin sounded the buzzer. Katrina started walking away from the buzzer then stopped as soon as she could no longer hear it.

She stopped 3 m from material A, 5 m away from material B, 2 m away from material C and 6 m away from material D.

a) Fill in the table below to show these results.

(4)

b) Which material, A, B, C or D was best at muffling sound? ....

(1)

c) How could you make the results more reliable?

....

(1)

d) Name an actual material that is good at muffling sound.

....

(1)

e) Write down **one** way in which we could use a material that is effective at muffling sound.

....

(1)

4 a) In 'Western' films, the scouts can warn other cowboys when horses are approaching, before they can actually see them.

Explain how the scouts can hear the horses from so far away.

....

....
(2)

b) A small battery-operated radio is turned on, then sealed in a plastic bag. It is lowered carefully into a bowl of water so that it is completely under the surface.

No water gets in the bag.

Describe what you would hear, from the time the radio is switched on to the time it is under the water.

....

....
(2)

c) Which **one** of these statements is true?

Tick the box by the correct answer.

☐ Sound cannot travel through solids.

☐ Sound can only travel through gases.

☐ Sound can travel through liquids.

(1)

CHANGING SOUNDS

Mark scheme

1	a)	Sound of voice makes string vibrate.	1 mark
		Vibration is passed along the string.	1 mark
	b)	Vibrations are larger. (Allow 'Vibrates more.')	1 mark
	c)	Vibration isn't passed along the string.	1 mark
2	a)	bottle A	1 mark
	b)	air (column)	1 mark
	c)	band A	1 mark
	d)	Pluck/pull the band harder/further.	1 mark
	e)	ruler C	1 mark

3 a)

Material	Distance (m)
A	3
B	5
C	2
D	6

correct headings		1 mark
'Material' in first column and 'Distance' in second column.		1 mark
Data entered correctly.		2 marks

	b)	material C	1 mark
	c)	Repeat tests.	1 mark
	d)	any good sound insulator	1 mark
	e)	any use for sound insulation eg ear defenders/between walls	1 mark
4	a)	Put ear to ground,	1 mark
		vibrations from hooves travelled along the surface.	1 mark
	b)	Sound gets slightly quieter when wrapped in bag.	1 mark
		Sound gets much quieter (but must still be audible) in water.	1 mark
	c)	Sound can travel through liquids.	1 mark

TOTAL: 22 marks

CHANGING SOUNDS

Recording teacher assessment using QCA Schemes of work

Class/year group: ....   Teacher: ....

The majority of pupils have met the learning outcomes as stated in the medium-term plans from this QCA unit and they can:

- generalise that sounds are produced when objects vibrate
- suggest how to change the pitch and loudness of the sounds produced by a range of musical instruments
- recognise that sounds travel through solids, water and air
- suggest how to investigate how well sound travels through different materials and say how good their evidence is.

+

Some have made more progress and can also:

- describe ways in which the pitch of a sound made by a particular instrument or vibrating object can be raised or lowered and identify what is vibrating in a range of musical instruments.

Names or initials
(Include explanatory notes as necessary.)

−

Some have not made this much progress but can:

- suggest ways of producing sounds
- distinguish between pitch and loudness, and suggest how to change the sound made by an instrument.

Names or initials
(Include explanatory notes as necessary.)

The back of this sheet is on page 144.

CHANGING SOUNDS

My concept map

Name ....

Look at the words below. Link the boxes together and label the lines, explaining your links.

You might want to cut the boxes out and arrange them yourself on a clean piece of paper.

You could draw your own concept map, using the same words.

| vibration |

| air | | ear |

| guitar string | | pitch |

| sound |

CHANGING SOUNDS

Complete the diagram

Draw labelled arrows on the diagrams below to show how sound gets from the bell to Jack's ear.

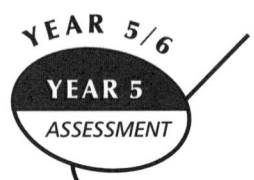

END-OF-YEAR ASSESSMENT QUESTIONS

Name .... Class .... Date ....

1 Your heart is an important organ in your body.

a) i) What job does your heart do in your body?

....
(1)

ii) How is your heart protected against damage inside your body? Fill in the missing word in the sentence below.

The heart is protected by your ....
(1)

b) The Year 5 football team had just finished a game.

Jason was star of the match. He had worked very hard for the team.

Describe **three** ways that Jason's running would affect his body by the end of the match.

1 ....

2 ....

3 ....
(3)

2 Look at the diagram of the inside of a flower, drawn below.

a) Choose words from this box to label the flower.

| sepal | ovary | stigma | stamen | petal | style |

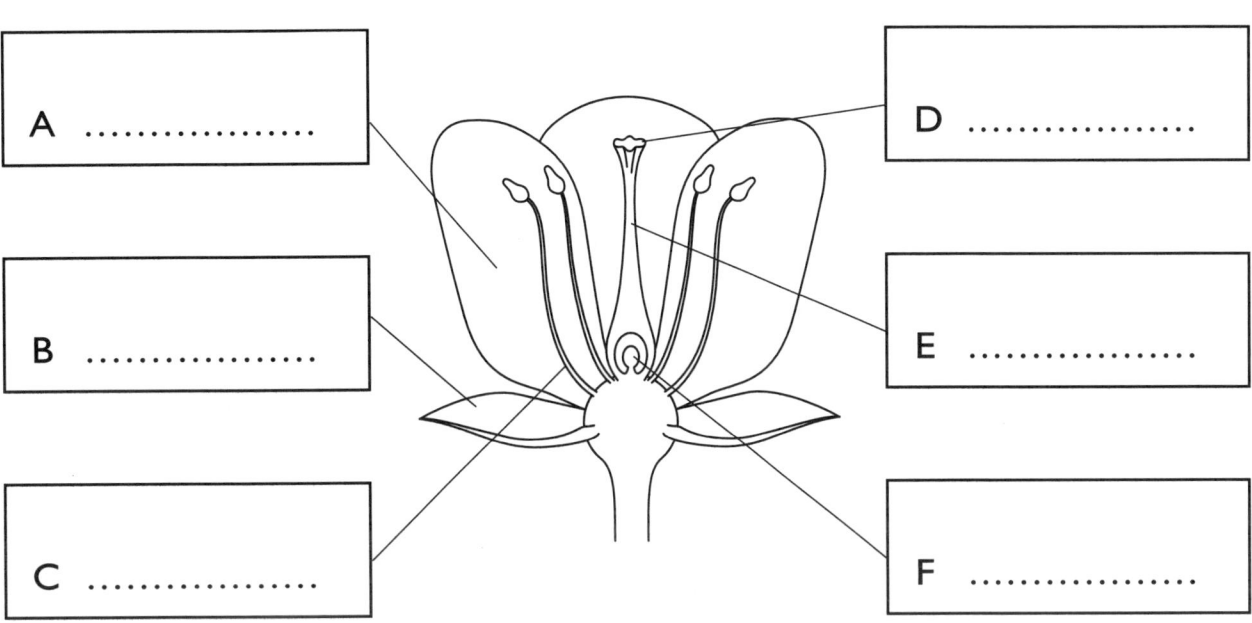

A ....

B ....

C ....

D ....

E ....

F ....

(6)

b) Complete the sentences below to describe what each part of the flower does.

    i) The stamen ....

(1)

    ii) The stigma ....

(1)

    iii) The petal ....

(1)

3 a) Here are some properties of solids, liquids and gases.

Next to each property, write down whether it describes a solid, a liquid or a gas.

Property	Solid, liquid or gas
Keeps its own shape.	
Can be squashed quite easily.	
Can flow in all directions.	

(3)

b) Look at the drawing of the bottle of perfume below.

Explain what happens when the top is taken off the bottle.

....

....

(2)

c) Draw a ring around each of the gases, at room temperature, in the list below.

brass   helium   oxygen

alcohol   carbon dioxide   diesel

(3)

4 A class was investigating what happens to a bowl of water when it is left on a windowsill. The children measured the water level every two days. Their results are shown in the table on the right.

Time (days)	Height of water in bowl (mm)
0	55
2	50
4	47
6	41
8	32
10	24

Use the grid below to draw a line graph to show their results.

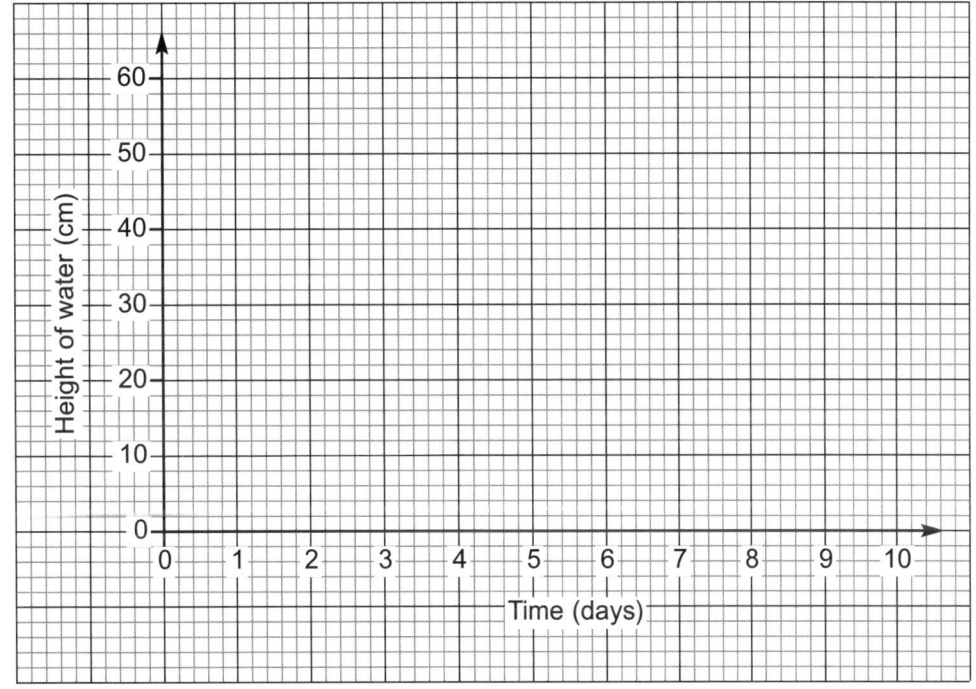

(7)

c) Explain why the water level dropped in the bowl.

....
(1)

d) Why do you think the graph is not a straight line?

....
(1)

e) How does the height of water depend on the time for which it stands?

....
....
(2)

5 a) Label the diagram below to show which part of the Earth is in daylight and which is at night time.
(The diagram is not drawn to scale.)

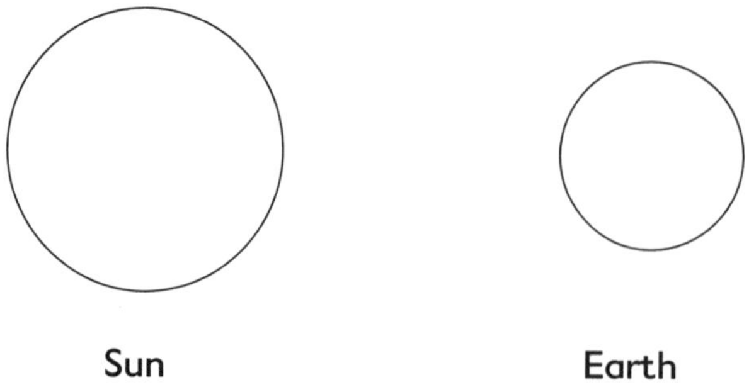

Sun   Earth

(2)

b) How will the diagram be different (if at all) in 24 hours' time?

....

(1)

c) Which of these statements are true?

Tick the boxes by the correct answers.

☐ The Earth is bigger than the Sun.

☐ The Earth is bigger than the Moon.

☐ The Sun is bigger than the Earth.

☐ The Earth orbits the Sun.

☐ The Sun orbits the Earth.

☐ The Earth orbits the Moon.

☐ The Moon orbits the Earth

☐ It takes the Earth 24 hours to spin around its axis once.

☐ It takes the Earth 28 days to spin around its axis once.

☐ It takes the Earth 1 year to spin around its axis once.

(4)

6 Ben can make a sound by blowing across the top of a bottle.

a) How can Ben make the sound from the bottle louder?

....
(1)

b) How can he make a sound with a higher pitch by blowing across the bottle?

....
(1)

c) Write the missing word to finish this sentence.

When we make a sound, something always v........................... .
(1)

d) Three identical elastic bands were plucked.

band A

band B

band C

Which band, A, B or C, made the sound with the highest pitch?

....
(1)

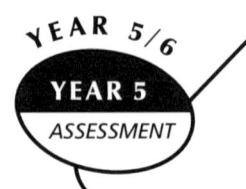

END-OF-YEAR ASSESSMENT QUESTIONS

Mark scheme

1 a) i) Pumps blood around the body. — 1 mark
   ii) ribs — 1 mark

   b) Get hot. — 1 mark
   Heart beats faster/higher pulse rate. — 1 mark
   Breathe faster. (Allow 'Feel tired.') — 1 mark

2 a) A: petal — 1 mark
   B: sepal — 1 mark
   C: stamen — 1 mark
   D: stigma — 1 mark
   E: style — 1 mark
   F: ovary — 1 mark

   b) i) makes pollen — 1 mark
   ii) pollen sticks to it — 1 mark
   iii) attracts insects — 1 mark

3 a) solid — 1 mark
   gas — 1 mark
   gas — 1 mark

   b) The smell of perfume spreads out/escapes from bottle — 1 mark
   as it evaporates/mixes with the air. — 1 mark

   c) oxygen — 1 mark
   carbon dioxide — 1 mark
   helium — 1 mark

4 a) 55 mm (units needed for mark) — 1 mark

   b) 1 mark for each correctly plotted point — 6 marks
   points joined with line — 1 mark

   c) The water evaporated. — 1 mark

   d) Some days hotter than others. — 1 mark

   e) The longer the bowl is left the lower the height of the water. — 2 marks
   (only 1 mark for specific example e.g. 'The height is low when it has been left a long time.')

5 a) 1 mark for part of Earth facing Sun labelled day
   1 mark for side facing away labelled night — 2 marks

   b) The same/no difference — 1 mark

   c) The Earth is bigger than the Moon. — 1 mark
   The Sun is bigger than the Earth. — 1 mark
   The Earth orbits the Sun. — 1 mark
   The Moon orbits the Earth. — 1 mark
   It takes the Earth 24 hours to spin around its axis once. — 1 mark

6 a) Blow harder. — 1 mark
   b) Add water. — 1 mark
   c) vibrates — 1 mark
   d) C — 1 mark

TOTAL: 46 marks

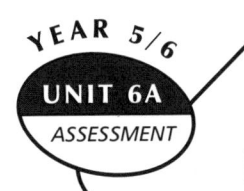

PLANTS AND ANIMALS IN THE ENVIRONMENT

Pupil checklist

By the end of this unit:

I should know that:

- [ ] green plants need light to grow well
- [ ] green plants make new plant material, using a gas from the air (carbon dioxide) and water, and this happens in their leaves when the plant is in sunlight
- [ ] plants need a small amount of nutrients from the soil to grow well
- [ ] nutrients, dissolved in water, are absorbed by the roots
- [ ] the roots, as well as absorbing water, anchor the plant in the soil
- [ ] fertilisers add nutrients to the soil
- [ ] animals and plants in a habitat depend on each other to survive
- [ ] food chains show who eats what in a habitat
- [ ] food chains begin with a plant (called the producer)
- [ ] different plants grow well in different soil conditions
- [ ] different animals and plants are found in different habitats.

I should be able to:

- [ ] make careful observations of plants growing, and use my scientific ideas to to explain them
- [ ] use a key to identify animals and plants
- [ ] explain how animals and plants are suited to their environments
- [ ] make detailed observations of soils
- [ ] draw conclusions from my observations of soil and use my scientific ideas to explain them
- [ ] draw food chains for a particular habitat.

Science Assessment Y5/6   © Lawrie Ryan, Nelson Thornes Ltd. 2002

PLANTS AND ANIMALS IN THE ENVIRONMENT

Assessment questions

Name .... **Class** .... **Date** ....

1 a) After a plant was kept in a cupboard for two weeks it looked like this.

Then it was kept on a windowsill for the next month and watered regularly.

Draw a picture in the box to show how the plant looked after this.

(3)

b) What difference would you notice between the colour of the leaves just after the plant was taken out from the cupboard, and after it had been on the windowsill for a time?

....
(1)

Science Assessment Y5/6   © Lawrie Ryan, Nelson Thornes Ltd. 2002

2 A gardener adds some fertiliser to her soil.

a) Explain how the plants take in the useful materials from the fertiliser.

....

....
(2)

b) Besides nutrients, what else must a plant take in to make new material and grow?

.... and ....
(2)

c) In which part of a plant does it make its own 'food for growth'?

....
(1)

d) Which **one** of these statements is true?

Tick the box by the correct answer.

☐ Plants suck up soil which is turned into new plant material.

☐ Plants absorb small amounts of nutrients from the soil to help them grow.

☐ Plants only use soil as a base to keep them steady.

(1)

3 Look at these pictures of animals and the key below them.

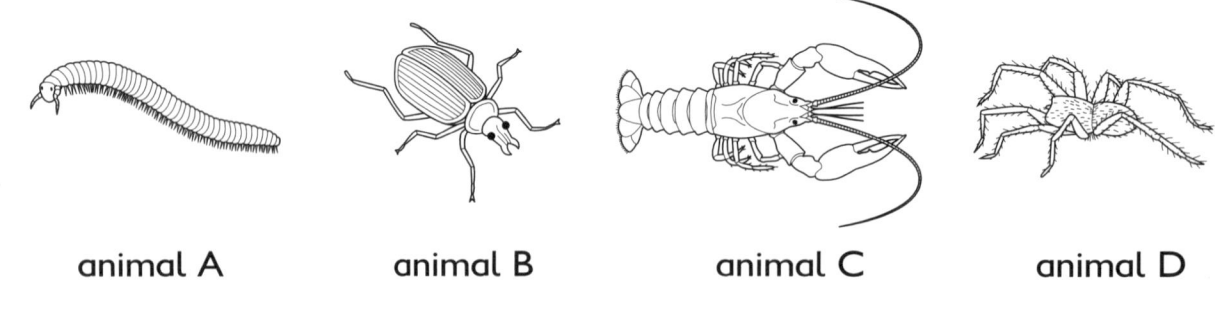

animal A   animal B   animal C   animal D

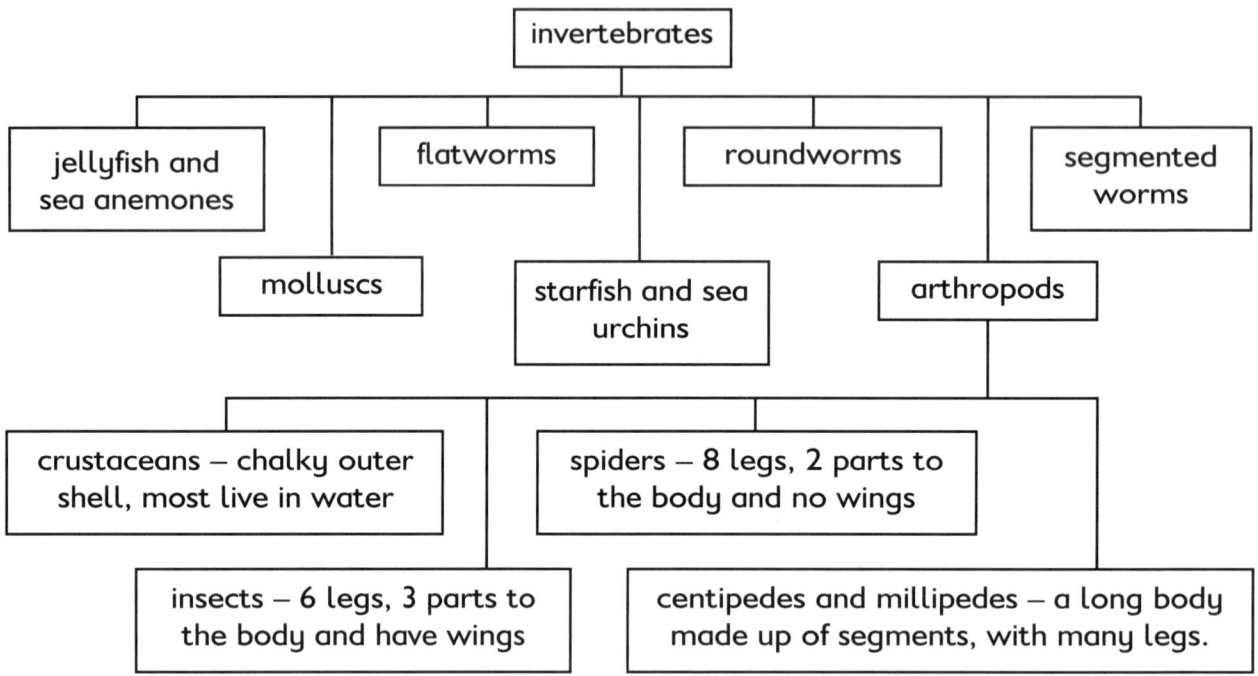

a) Complete the sentence below.

Animals A, B, C and D are all types of ....
(1)

b) Use the key to identify the specific group of animals to which A, B, C and D belong.

   i)   Animal A belongs to the group of ....

   ii) Animal B belongs to the group of ....

   iii) Animal C belongs to the group of ....

   iv) Animal D belongs to the group of ....
(4)

4 a) Write down **two** ways in which animals depend on plants.

   1 ....

   2 ....
   (2)

b) Write down **two** ways in which plants depend on animals.

   1 ....

   2 ....
   (2)

c) Read the following information.

   Greenfly are not popular insects with gardeners as they feed on and damage rose bushes. You can get rid of greenfly by spraying the roses with pesticide. But organic rose growers release ladybirds on their rose bushes as these enjoy a good meal of greenfly!

   i) Draw a food chain from the information given above.

   .... ➜ .... ➜ ....
   (3)

   ii) If the arrows above were replaced by words, what would the words be?

   ....
   (1)

   iii) Name the producer in the food chain above.

   ....
   (1)

d) Draw a food chain to connect the animals and plant in the box below.

   | weasel   fox   grass   rabbit |

   .... ➜ .... ➜ .... ➜ ....
   (4)

5 Look at the three types of soil drawn below.

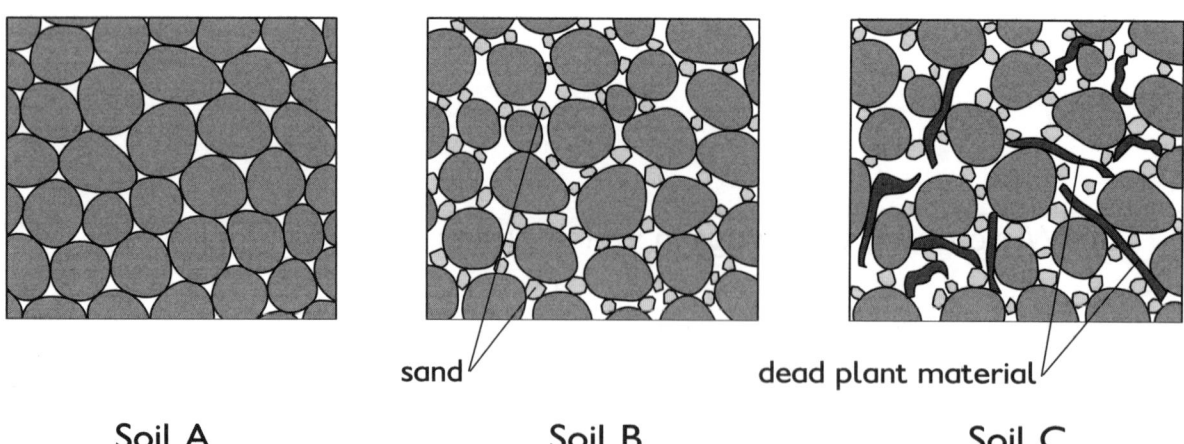

Soil A   Soil B   Soil C

a) Which type of soil, A, B or C, is best suited to animals that live mainly underground?

....
(1)

b) Give **two** reasons why animals would do well in this soil (from part (a)).

1 ....

....

2 ....

....
(2)

c) Give **two** reasons why plants would grow well in this soil. (from part (a)).

1 ....

....

2 ....

....
(2)

6 Look at this picture of a wading bird.

Write down **two** ways in which this bird is adapted to its environment.

Explain your reasoning in each case.

1 ....

....

2 ....

....

(4)

PLANTS AND ANIMALS IN THE ENVIRONMENT

Mark scheme

1	a)	Drawing to show:	
		more leaves	1 mark
		taller/more upright	1 mark
		thicker stem	1 mark
	b)	They would be greener after a period on the windowsill.	1 mark
2	a)	dissolves in water	1 mark
		taken in/absorbed through roots	1 mark
	b)	air (carbon dioxide) and water	2 marks
	c)	leaves	1 mark
	d)	Plants absorb small amounts of nutrients from the soil to help them grow.	1 mark
3	a)	invertebrate/arthropod	1 mark
	b)	A: millipede/centipede	1 mark
		B: insect	1 mark
		C: crustacean	1 mark
		D: spider	1 mark
4	a)	two examples such as food/shelter/shade	2 marks
	b)	two examples such as nutrients for soil/disperse seeds	2 marks
	c)	i) rose (bush) → greenfly → ladybird	3 marks
		ii) (is) eaten (consumed) by	1 mark
		iii) rose (bush)	1 mark
	d)	grass → rabbit → weasel → fox	4 marks
5	a)	soil C	1 mark
	b)	Air in soil can travel/get through soil more easily. Food from decaying plants available. any two reasons	2 marks
	c)	Roots can push through soil. Nutrients in soil from dead plant material. Water can get to roots more easily. any two reasons	2 marks
6		1 mark for each adaptation and 1 mark for each reason, for example: long legs (1) to wade in shallow water (1) long beak (1) to burrow into mud for food (1) webbed feet (1) for swimming/not sinking into mud (1).	4 marks

TOTAL: 37 marks

YEAR 5/6 UNIT 6A ASSESSMENT

PLANTS AND ANIMALS IN THE ENVIRONMENT

Recording teacher assessment using QCA Schemes of work

Class/year group: ……………………   Teacher: ……………………………………

The majority of pupils have met the learning outcomes as stated in the medium-term plans from this QCA unit and they can:

- recognise that a green plant needs light and water to grow well and that it produces new material from air and water
- describe how animals in two habitats are suited to conditions
- represent feeding relationships in food chains beginning with a green plant
- use keys to identify animals and plants.

+

Some have made more progress and can also:

- recognise that green plants are the source of food for all animals
- explain that plants produce material for new growth from air and water in the presence of sunlight

Names or initials
(Include explanatory notes as necessary.)

−

Some have not made this much progress but can:

- recognise that a green plant needs light and water to grow well
- state that animals and plants live in different habitats
- state that some animals feed on other animals and some on plants
- use keys to identify some animals and plants.

Names or initials
(Include explanatory notes as necessary.)

The back of this sheet is on page 144.

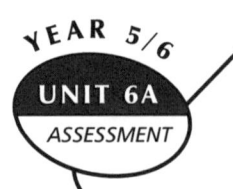

PLANTS AND ANIMALS IN THE ENVIRONMENT

My concept map

Name ....

Look at the words below. Link the boxes together and label the lines, explaining your links.

You might want to cut the boxes out and arrange them yourself on a clean piece of paper.

You could draw your own concept map, using the same words.

| prey |

| predator | | animals |

| plants | | adapted |

| producer |

PLANTS AND ANIMALS IN THE ENVIRONMENT

Complete the diagram

Draw labelled arrows on the diagrams below to show how the plant feeds so that it can grow new plant material.

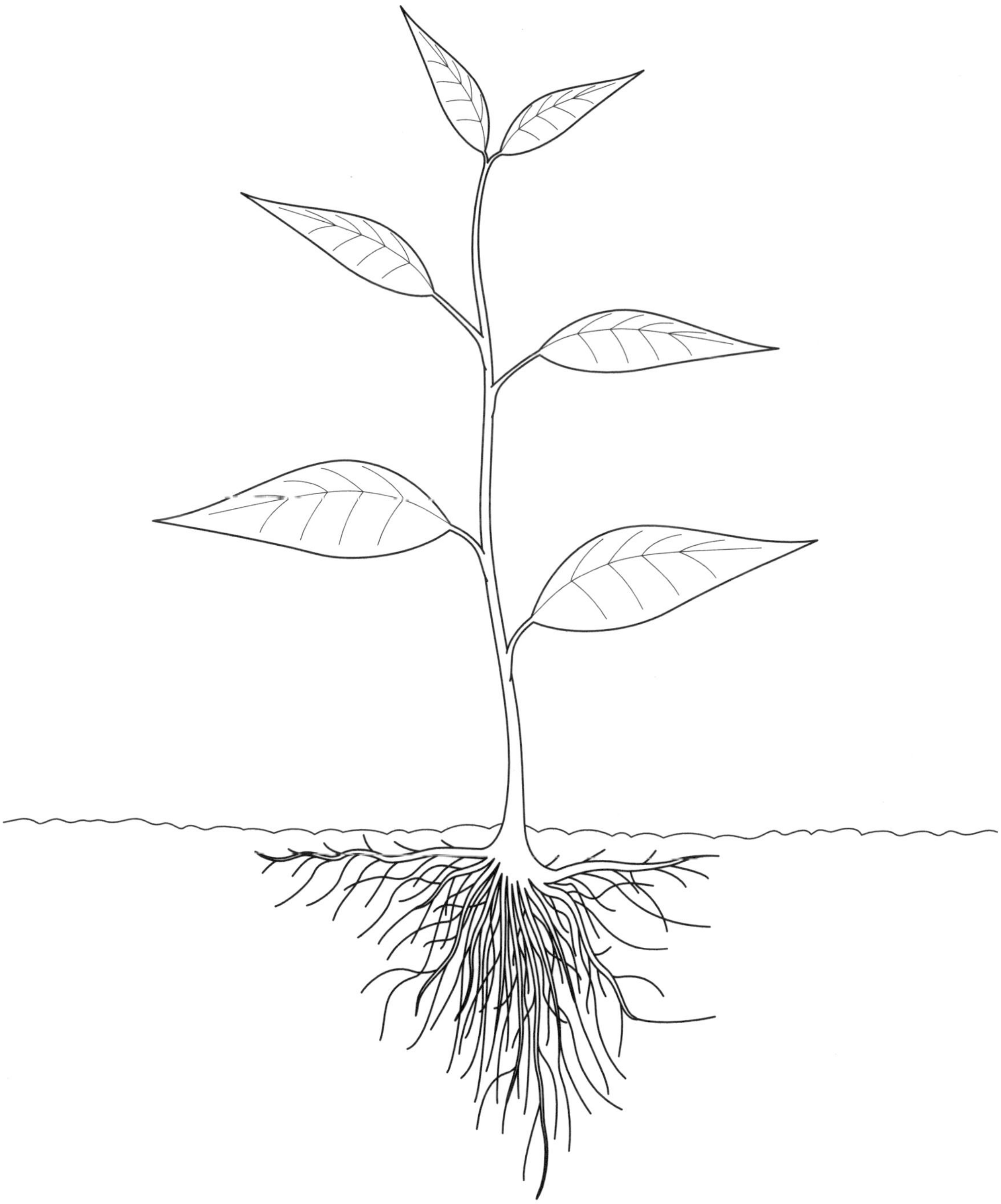

MICRO-ORGANISMS

Pupil checklist

By the end of this unit:

I should know that:

- [ ] very small organisms are called micro-organisms (or microbes) and that some of these are harmful
- [ ] micro-organisms are often too small to be seen without a microscope
- [ ] micro-organisms can cause food to decay
- [ ] food needs to be handled and stored with care
- [ ] micro-organisms bring about decay in nature and they are living things
- [ ] decay can be a good thing in nature
- [ ] micro-organisms feed and grow
- [ ] micro-organisms are useful in food production.

I should be able to:

- [ ] consider the reasons for some common illnesses
- [ ] make suggestions about observing food in experiments, bearing in mind the need for safety
- [ ] make suggestions about what yeast needs to grow
- [ ] make careful observations of yeast and compare these to draw conclusions about the effect of yeast on dough
- [ ] use scientific ideas to explain my conclusions.

YEAR 5/6
UNIT 6B
ASSESSMENT

MICRO-ORGANISMS

Assessment questions

Name .... Class .... Date ....

1 Read this information then answer the questions.

> A few hundred years ago, smallpox was a disease that killed many people. It could be passed on easily between people and there was an epidemic in England in 1796.
>
> Edward Jenner noticed that farm workers who looked after cows never caught smallpox. They were exposed to a much less serious disease called cowpox. Edward had the idea that cowpox could somehow protect people from getting the deadly smallpox.
>
> He decided to try out a very dangerous experiment. He persuaded a local farmer to let his son be infected with cowpox. He promised the farmer that this would protect the boy against smallpox. Edward collected some puss from one of the sores on a milk-maid with cowpox. He put the puss into the young boy by scratching his arm and smearing the liquid on to the cuts. Sure enough, the boy had a mild attack of cowpox.
>
> Six weeks later Edward did the same thing to the farmer's son, but this time with puss from a smallpox sore. Fortunately, Edward's theory was correct and the boy did not catch smallpox.

a) Smallpox is an infectious disease. What does this mean?

....
(1)

b) What are the tiny living things that cause smallpox called?

....
(1)

c) What evidence did Edward Jenner base his experiment on?

....
(1)

Science Assessment Y5/6   © Lawrie Ryan, Nelson Thornes Ltd. 2002

2 Dentists recommend that we brush our teeth at least twice a day.

a) Why does brushing your teeth regularly help to prevent tooth decay?

....

....
(1)

b) Complete the following sentence.

Brushing your teeth regularly also protects you against disease of the ....
(1)

c) What type of micro-organism grows on bread that is left out for too long?

....
(1)

d) Complete the following sentences.

i) People who eat food that has harmful micro-organisms growing on it can get food ....

ii) The food itself d.............. in the process.
(2)

e) Make a list of **three** safety rules to keep your kitchen hygienic.

1 ....

2 ....

3 ....
(3)

3 a) What does the word 'decompose' mean?

　..

　..
　　　　　　　　　　　　　　　　　　　　　　　　　　　　　　　　(1)

b) Which of these things are decomposed by micro-organisms?

　Draw a ring around each one of your answers.

| newspaper | biodegradable plastic | tin can | non-biodegradable plastic |

| block of concrete | grass cuttings | wooden board | vegetable peelings |

　　　　　　　　　　　　　　　　　　　　　　　　　　　　　　　　(4)

c) How do the micro-organisms decompose materials?

　..

　..
　　　　　　　　　　　　　　　　　　　　　　　　　　　　　　　　(1)

d) Why would it be a problem to us if materials did **not** decay?

　..

　..

　..
　　　　　　　　　　　　　　　　　　　　　　　　　　　　　　　　(1)

4 Bakers know just the right amount of ingredients to make the best bread.

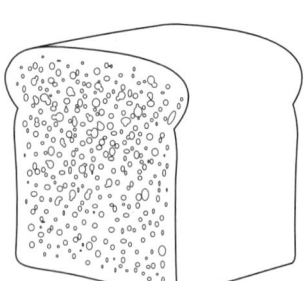

a) Which micro-organism do bakers add to their mixture to make it rise?

....
(1)

b) What does the micro-organism feed on to make the mixture rise?

....
(1)

c) What other conditions are needed for the bread dough-mixture to rise?

....
(1)

d) How can you tell when the dough-mixture has risen?

....
(1)

e) What is the last thing you must to do when you are making bread?

....
(1)

f) Write down **two** other foods that are made using micro-organisms.

.... and ....
(2)

MICRO-ORGANISMS

Mark scheme

1	a)	Can spread to other people.	1 mark
	b)	germs/micro-organisms/virus	1 mark
	c)	That milkmaids that had had cowpox did not catch smallpox.	1 mark
2	a)	removes micro-organisms/bacteria from teeth/mouth/gums	1 mark
	b)	gums	1 mark
	c)	mould/fungus	1 mark
	d)	poisoning	1 mark
		decays/decomposes	1 mark
	e)	Accept any three rules, for example: Clean work surfaces thoroughly. Use different knives for raw and cooked meat. Cook food thoroughly.	3 marks
3	a)	decay/break down	1 mark
	b)	newspaper	1 mark
		biodegradable plastic	1 mark
		vegetable peelings	1 mark
		grass cuttings	1 mark
		(Take 1 mark off for each incorrect answer included.)	
	c)	They feed on them.	1 mark
	d)	Rubbish would build up/last forever/no space to get rid of it.	1 mark
4	a)	yeast	1 mark
	b)	sugar/glucose	1 mark
	c)	warmth	1 mark
	d)	Bubbles trapped in mixture/it expands/gets bigger.	1 mark
	e)	Bake/heat it.	1 mark
	f)	cheese (1) yoghurt (1) (allow beer or wine)	2 marks

TOTAL: 25 marks

MICRO-ORGANISMS

Recording teacher assessment using QCA Schemes of work

Class/year group: .... Teacher: ....

The majority of pupils have met the learning outcomes as stated in the medium-term plans from this QCA unit and they can:

- recognise that there are many very small organisms which can cause illness or decay or which can be used in food production and that these micro-organisms feed, grow and reproduce like other organisms.

+	−
Some have made more progress and can also: • describe evidence that yeast is living • explain how micro-organisms can move from one food source to another and how this can cause food poisoning.	**Some have not made this much progress but can:** • recognise that very small living can cause illness.
Names or initials (Include explanatory notes as necessary.)	**Names or initials** (Include explanatory notes as necessary.)

The back of this sheet is on page 144.

Science Assessment Y5/6 © Lawrie Ryan, Nelson Thornes Ltd. 2002

MICRO-ORGANISMS

My concept map

Name ....

Look at the words below. Link the boxes together and label the lines, explaining your links.

You might want to cut the boxes out and arrange them yourself on a clean piece of paper.

You could draw your own concept map, using the same words.

| micro-organism |

| yeast | | sugar |

| decompose | | food |

| disease |

MORE ABOUT DISSOLVING

Pupil checklist

By the end of this unit:

I should know that:

- [ ] solids that do not dissolve in water can be separated from water by filtering
- [ ] when solids dissolve we get a clear solution (that might also be coloured)
- [ ] a soluble solid cannot be separated from its solution by filtering
- [ ] when a liquid evaporates from a solution the solid is left behind
- [ ] when I repeat my readings I can have more trust in what they tell me

I should be able to:

- [ ] describe my method in a series of steps
- [ ] make predictions about which types of water contain dissolved materials, and test my predictions
- [ ] make predictions about what happens when water evaporates, and test my predictions
- [ ] turn my ideas about what makes a solid dissolve more quickly into a question I can investigate
- [ ] plan how to carry out a fair test, selecting the apparatus I will need
- [ ] make careful observations and measurements
- [ ] use a line graph to present my results
- [ ] make comparisons and draw conclusions
- [ ] evaluate a line graph by saying how well it shows the results of my experiments

Assessment questions

Name .... Class .... Date ....

1. Sara collected some water from a puddle and put it in a jam jar. She took the water back to class and filtered it.

a) Write down how you would filter a solution of dirty water, step by step.

....

....

....
(3)

b) What is separated from the dirty water by filtering it?

....
(1)

c) How could Sara prove that there are solids left in the water that has been filtered?

....

....
(2)

2 a) Some children in a class were investigating blue ink.

Their teacher heated some of the ink over a burner.

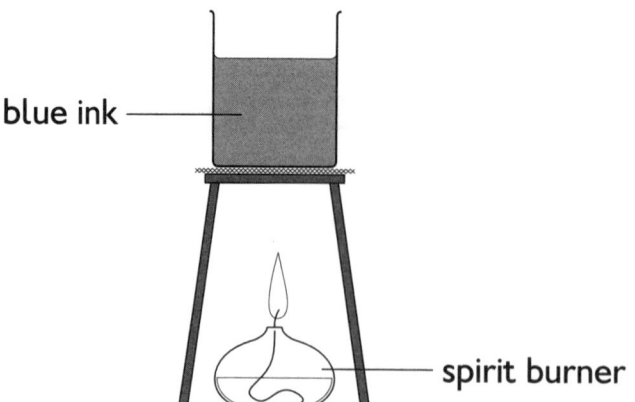

i) What would you see escaping from the surface of the ink?

....
(1)

ii) Why would you see this?

....
(1)

b) The teacher then brings a can with ice inside it near the ink as it is heated.

i) What would you see forming on the outside of the can?

....
(1)

ii) What do we call the process that takes place on the outside of the can?

....
(1)

3 A group of children were finding out how temperature affects the time it takes sugar to dissolve.

They wanted to make their test as fair as possible.

a) List **three** things that they should keep the same in each test.

1 ....

2 ....

3 ....
(3)

b) What should they change in each of their tests?

....
(1)

c) Their results are shown in the table below.

Temperature (°C)	Time to dissolve (seconds)
20	160
30	72
40	45
50	30
60	26

Use the grid on the next page to present these results on a graph.

d) Using your graph, say how temperature affects how quickly sugar dissolves.

....

....
(2)

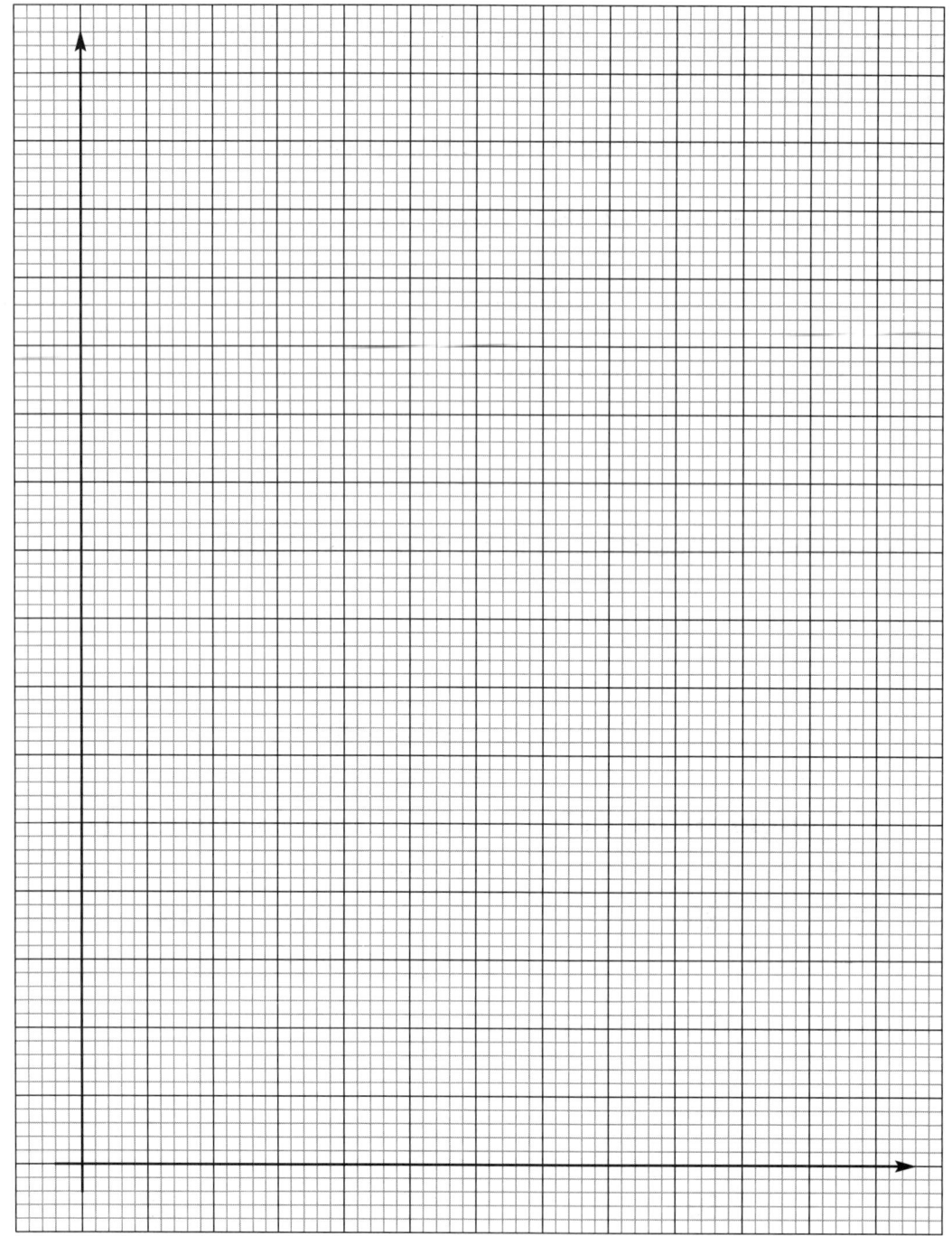

(9)

e) How could the group have made their results more reliable?

....

....

....

(1)

MORE ABOUT DISSOLVING

Mark scheme

1 a) Fold the filter paper. — 1 mark
Put the filter paper inside a funnel. — 1 mark
Pour dirty water into the funnel. — 1 mark

b) Insoluble solids/bits (particles) of soil (dirt) — 1 mark

c) Let the water evaporate — 1 mark
and see if any solid is left behind. — 1 mark
(Or 1 mark for 'looking at the colour of the water'
and 1 mark for saying that if it is not clear (colourless) there must
be something still in it.)

2 a) i) water (vapour)/steam — 1 mark
ii) The hot water evaporates/boils off. — 1 mark

b) i) drops of water (Allow 'condensation'.) — 1 mark
ii) condensation — 1 mark

3 a) three factors to control, for example, mass (amount) of sugar,
volume (amount) of water, rate of stirring, type of sugar — 3 marks

b) temperature — 1 mark

c) Vertical axis chosen for 'Time (to dissolve)',
horizontal axis chosen for 'Temperature' ('Temp'). — 1 mark
Both axes labelled correctly, including units. — 1 mark
Even scale chosen. — 1 mark
1 mark for each point correctly plotted. — 5 marks
Points joined by line (or line of best fit). — 1 mark

d) The higher the temperature, the more quickly sugar dissolves. — 2 marks
(only 1 mark for specific example, e.g. 'At high temperatures sugar
dissolves quickly.')

e) Repeat their tests. — 1 mark

TOTAL: 26 marks

YEAR 5/6 UNIT 6C ASSESSMENT

MORE ABOUT DISSOLVING

Recording teacher assessment using QCA Schemes of work

Class/year group: …………………… Teacher: …………………………………

The majority of pupils have met the learning outcomes as stated in the medium-term plans from this QCA unit and they can:

- recognise that solids remain in the solution when they dissolve and can be recovered by evaporation
- recognise that there is a limit to how much solid will dissolve in a liquid
- identify several factors that affect the rate at which a solid dissolves
- investigate an aspect of dissolving, presenting results obtained in a suitable graph and explaining what the results show.

+

Some have made more progress and can also:

- present results in a line graph where appropriate and explain why it is important to repeat measurements.

Names or initials
(Include explanatory notes as necessary.)

−

Some have not made this much progress but can:

- recognise that a solid can be recovered from a solution by evaporation
- with help, investigate an aspect of dissolving and present results in a suitable table.

Names or initials
(Include explanatory notes as necessary.)

The back of this sheet is on page 144.

MORE ABOUT DISSOLVING

My concept map

Name ....

Look at the words below. Link the boxes together and label the lines, explaining your links.

You might want to cut the boxes out and arrange them yourself on a clean piece of paper.

You could draw your own concept map, using the same words.

| water |

| sugar | | salt |

| chalk | | solution |

| evaporate |

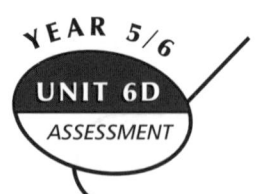

REVERSIBLE AND IRREVERSIBLE CHANGES

Pupil checklist

By the end of this unit:

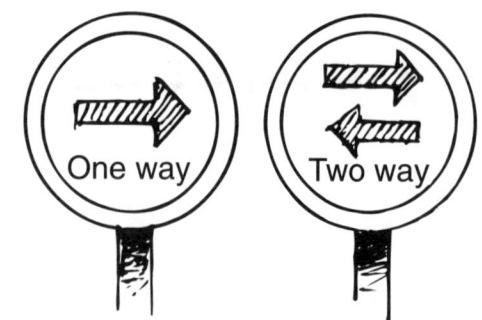

I should know that:

- [ ] mixing materials can cause them to change
- [ ] I can separate insoluble solids from a liquid by filtering
- [ ] I can get a solid from its solution by evaporating off the liquid
- [ ] some changes that happen when I mix materials cannot be easily reversed (turned back into what I started with)
- [ ] heating some materials causes them to change
- [ ] cooling some materials causes them to change
- [ ] we get new materials when we burn something and it is usually difficult to reverse the change.

I should be able to:

- [ ] make careful observations, record them and use my scientific ideas to explain them
- [ ] recognise and judge the risks and hazards when we burn materials.

REVERSIBLE AND IRREVERSIBLE CHANGES

Assessment questions

Name .... Class .... Date ....

1 a) A change may be reversible or irreversible.
What do we mean when we describe a change as 'reversible'?

....
(1)

Jason mixed some different powders with water. He recorded his results in a table like this the one.

Powder	Observations
A	Powder fizzed and eventually just a solution was left.
B	Made a thick gooey paste that set hard when left. The jar felt warm.
C	The blue powder dissolved and the water turned blue.
D	White crystals dissolved. The water didn't look like it had changed.

b) Use Jason's observations to fill in the table below. Enter 'yes' or 'no' for each change.

Change	Is this a reversible change?
A + water	
B + water	
C + water	
D + water	

(4)

c) Explain your **first** answer in the table.

....

....
(2)

Science Assessment Y5/6   © Lawrie Ryan, Nelson Thornes Ltd. 2002

2 Look at the changes in the diagrams below.

Write 'reversible' or 'irreversible' under each one.

a) chocolate

....

b)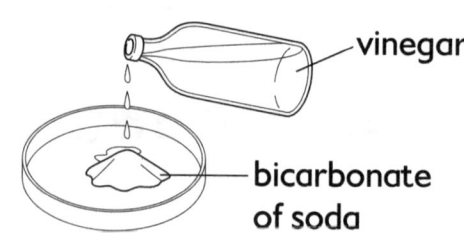

....

c) mixture of cement, sand and water

....

d)

....

(4)

3 a) Look at the drawing of a candle burning.

Use the idea of a burning candle to show the difference between reversible and irreversible changes.

....

....

....

....

....
(4)

b) The foam padding in this sofa has been treated to make it less likely to catch fire.

   i) How might a sofa catch fire?

   ....
   (1)

   ii) Why has the government banned certain types of plastic foam from being used in furniture?

   ....
   (1)

4 Zak's naughty young brother has mixed sand in with the salt in their kitchen.

How can Zak remove the sand and get back the pure salt?

Use the boxes below to draw a series of labelled diagrams to show how Zak can solve the problem in **three** steps.

Step 1

Step 2

Step 3

(3)

REVERSIBLE AND IRREVERSIBLE CHANGES

Mark scheme

1. a) A change in which we can easily get back what we started with.   1 mark

    b)

Change	Is this a reversible change?
A + water	no
B + water	no
C + water	yes
D + water	yes

    4 marks

    c) A new material (the gas) is made   1 mark
    that can't easily be changed back into A and water.   1 mark

2. a) reversible   1 mark
    b) irreversible   1 mark
    c) irreversible   1 mark
    d) reversible   1 mark

3. a) Look for the following points:
    wax melts   1 mark
    turns back to solid wax – reversible change   1 mark
    wax burns   1 mark
    forming gases that can't be changed back to wax – irreversible   1 mark

    b) i) Accept any sensible answer, for example, a lighted cigarette.   1 mark
    ii) They gave off poisonous/toxic gases/fumes.   1 mark

4. Diagrams to show:
    Step 1 – add water and stir   1 mark
    Step 2 – filtering the mixture   1 mark
    Step 3 – evaporate off water (allow heating or leaving for some time.   1 mark
    (Take 1 mark off if diagrams are not labelled.)

    TOTAL: 20 marks

YEAR 5/6 UNIT 6D ASSESSMENT

REVERSIBLE AND IRREVERSIBLE CHANGES

Recording teacher assessment using QCA Schemes of work

Class/year group: .... **Teacher:** ....

The majority of pupils have met the learning outcomes as stated in the medium-term plans from this QCA unit and they can:

- use careful observation to describe a number of changes
- classify some changes, e.g. dissolving, as reversible and others, e.g burning, as irreversible
- recognise that irreversible changes often make new and useful materials and recognise the hazards of burning materials.

+

Some have made more progress and can also:

- explain that in some cases the new materials made are gases and identify some evidence, e.g. vigorous bubbling, for the production of gases.

Names or initials
(Include explanatory notes as necessary.)

−

Some have not made this much progress but can:

- use careful observation to describe a number of changes and identify whether some changes are reversible or not.

Names or initials
(Include explanatory notes as necessary.)

The back of this sheet is on page 144.

Science Assessment Y5/6   © Lawrie Ryan, Nelson Thornes Ltd. 2002

YEAR 5/6 UNIT 6D ASSESSMENT

REVERSIBLE AND IRREVERSIBLE CHANGES

My concept map

Name ....

Look at the words below. Link the boxes together and label the lines, explaining your links.

You might want to cut the boxes out and arrange them yourself on a clean piece of paper.

You could draw your own concept map, using the same words.

| changes |

| reversible | | irreversible |

| melting | | condensation |

| burning |

FORCES IN ACTION

Pupil checklist

By the end of this unit:

I should know that:

- [ ] Earth and objects are pulled towards each other by a force called 'gravity', which causes objects to have weight
- [ ] weight is a force and is measured in units called 'newtons'
- [ ] several forces may act on one object
- [ ] when an object is placed in water, the water provides a force upwards on it, and this force is called the 'upthrust'
- [ ] the distance an elastic band stretches depends on the force acting on it
- [ ] air resistance slows down moving objects
- [ ] air resistance acts in the opposite direction to an object's weight.

I should be able to:

- [ ] measure forces carefully, using a forcemeter
- [ ] read different scales on a forcemeter
- [ ] represent the direction of forces by arrows
- [ ] use tables to present results
- [ ] spot patterns and draw conclusions from my results
- [ ] repeat measurements in order to check them
- [ ] evaluate repeated measures
- [ ] make careful measurements of length
- [ ] show data on a line graph and use it to spot patterns in the data
- [ ] use a line graph to describe how changing one factor affects a falling spinner.

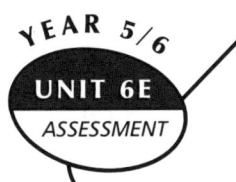

FORCES IN ACTION

Assessment questions

Name .... Class .... Date ....

1 a) Imagine Sam standing at different places around the world. Sam is holding a yo-yo at the end of its string. The yo-yo is shown in the top picture. Draw in the string and yo-yo in the other **three** places.

(3)

b) There is a downward force that acts on the floor under any object.

Complete the following sentence.

The downward force on the floor is called the object's ....

(1)

c) What causes the force you named in b)?

....

(1)

d) What would be the difference between the force in b) measured on the Moon and the same the force measured on Earth? Complete the following sentence.

The force would be .... on the Moon.

(1)

2 a) What are the units that are used to measure forces? ....
(1)

b) Write down the forces shown by the forcemeters below.

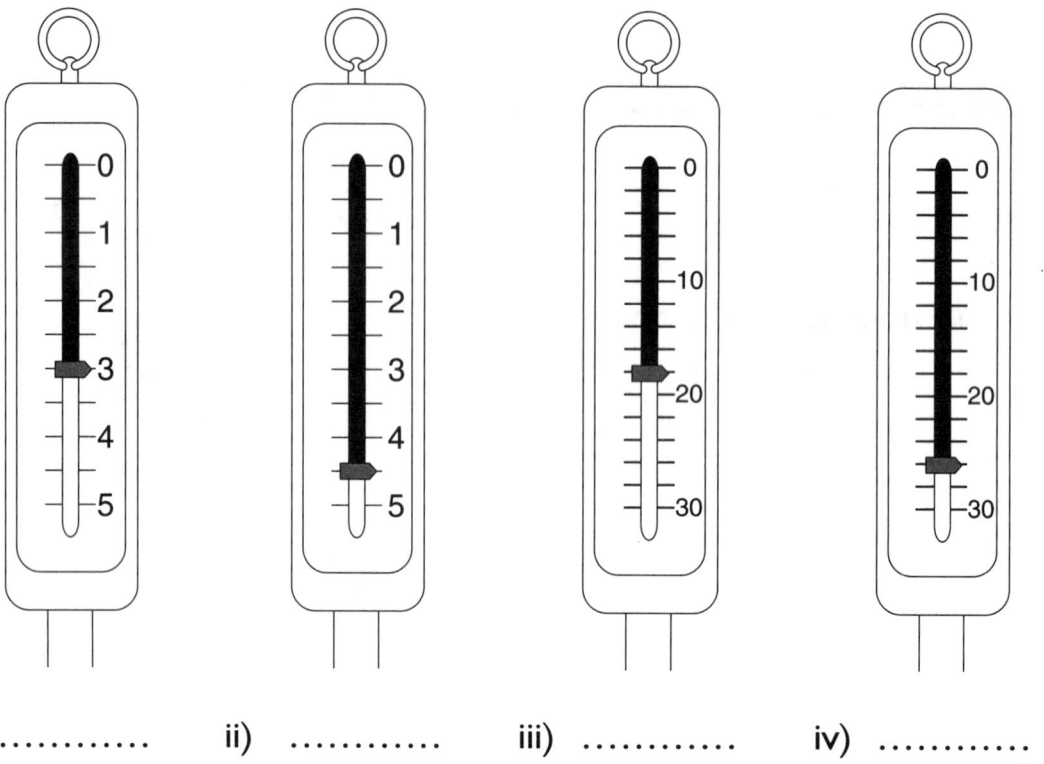

i) .... ii) .... iii) .... iv) ....
(4)

3 a) Hannah hung a block of metal from a forcemeter. Draw arrows on the diagram below, to show the forces acting on the block of metal.

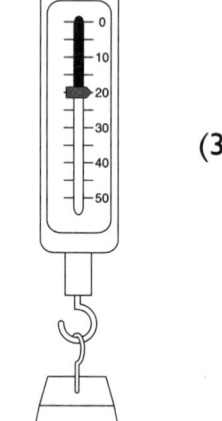

(3)

b) The metal block weighed 20 N. Hannah lowered the metal block into a bowl of water. When the metal block was under the surface, she read the forcemeter again.

   i) What do you think Hannah noticed about the reading on the forcemeter?

   ....
   (1)

   ii) Explain your answer.

   ....
   (1)

4. Some children were investigating elastic bands and forces. They attached a band to a fixed point, then they added masses to the free end of the band and measured its length each time.

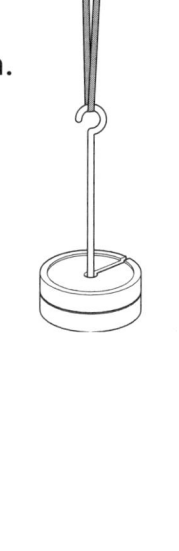

a) Their table of results is shown below. Fill in the last column.

Mass (g)	Length (cm)	Distance stretched from start of experiment (cm)
0	10	0
50	11.5	
100	13	
150	14.5	
200	15.9	

(4)

b) Use the grid below to show the mass and the distance stretched.

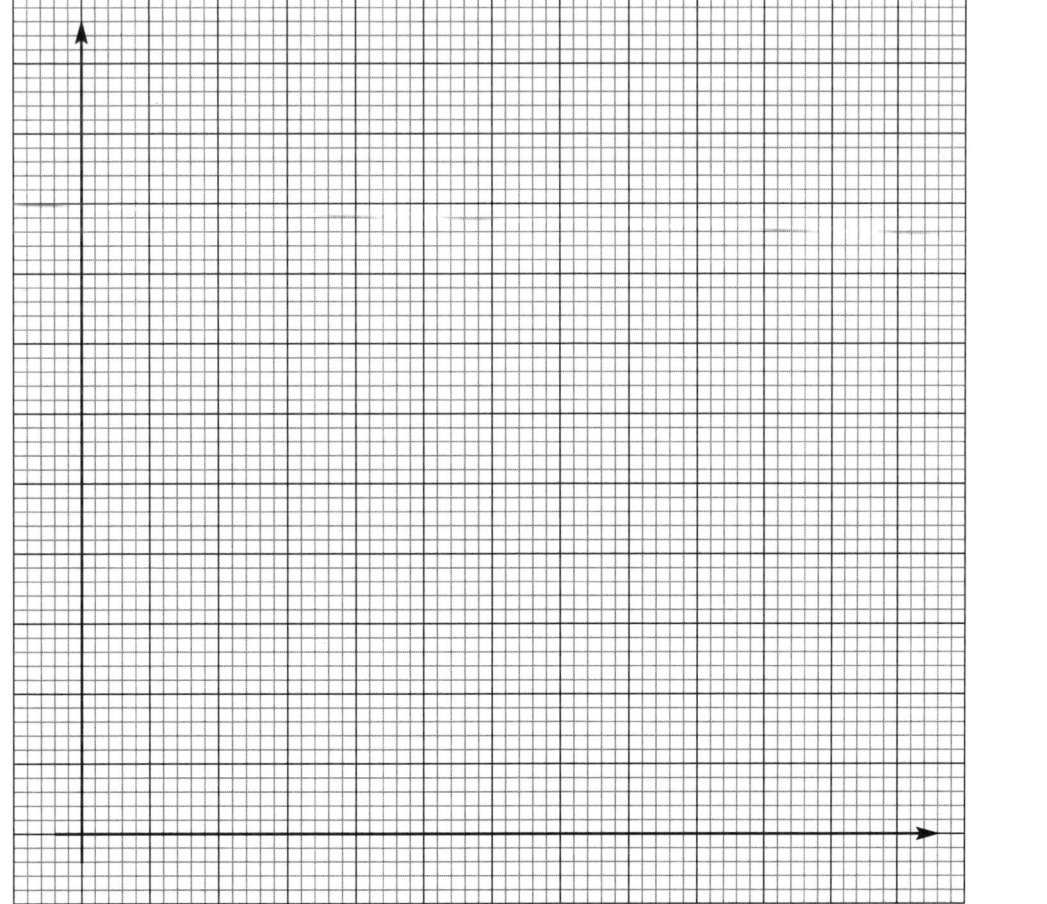

(6)

c) How does the force applied affect the distance the band stretches?

....

(2)

5 A group of children were investigating paper spinners. They decide to see if the length of its wings affected how long it took to fall. They repeated each test three times.

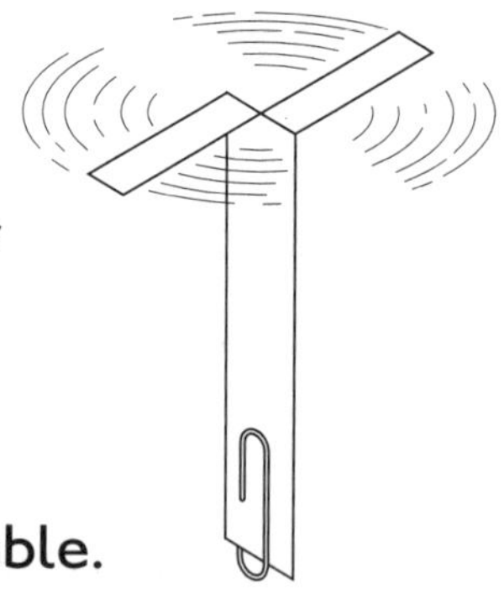

a) Their table of results is shown below. Work out the mean (average) results for the last column of their table.

Length of wings (cm)	Time for spinner to hit the floor (seconds)			
	First try	Second try	Third try	Mean (average)
2	1.23	1.33	0.77	
3	1.56	1.38	1.32	
4	1.75	1.88	1.59	
5	2.09	1.98	1.99	

(4)

b) Why was it a good idea to repeat their readings?

....
(1)

c) Which reading would you have least confidence in? Explain why.

....

....
(2)

d) What would be the best way to display these results on a graph?

Tick the box.   ☐ bar chart   ☐ line graph   (1)

e) What is the pattern in the data?

....
(2)

f) Explain the pattern in the data.

....

....
(2)

FORCES IN ACTION

Mark scheme

1 a) 1 mark for each yo-yo hanging towards centre of Earth — 3 marks
    b) weight — 1 mark
    c) gravity/attraction between Earth and object — 1 mark
    d) smaller/less/lower/decreased — 1 mark

2 a) newtons — 1 mark
       same size/shape glasses — 1 mark
    b) i) 3 N — 1 mark
       ii) 4.5 N — 1 mark
       iii) 18 N — 1 mark
       iv) 26 N — 1 mark
    (Take 1 mark off if no units are included.)

3 a) arrow pointing upwards from block — 1 mark
       arrow pointing downwards from block — 1 mark
       both arrows same size — 1 mark
    (Take 1 mark off for each extra arrow included.)
    b) i) lower/less/smaller — 1 mark
       ii) mention of upthrust from water — 1 mark

4 a) 1 mark each for 1.5, 3(.0), 4.5, 5.9 — 4 marks
    b) Correctly labelled axes, including units — 1 mark
       even scale — 1 mark
       Vertical axis: 'Distance band stretches (cm)' and horizontal axis: 'Mass (g)'. — 1 mark
       Points plotted correctly. — 2 marks
       Points joined by line. — 1 mark
    c) The larger the force, the further the elastic band stretches. — 2 marks
    (only 1 mark for specific example, e.g. 'A large force stretches the band a long way.')

5 a) 1 mark each for 1.11, 1.42, 1.74, 2.02 — 4 marks
    b) Because the times were so short it is difficult to be accurate — 1 mark
    c) The first set — 1 mark
       because they have the biggest differences/shortest time gives biggest error in timings. — 1 mark
    d) line graph — 1 mark
    e) The larger/longer the wings, the slower/longer it takes the spinner to fall. — 2 marks
    (only 1 mark for specific example, e.g. 'Spinners with big wings take longer to fall.')
    f) Larger wings have more air under them — 1 mark
       so have greater upward force acting on them. — 1 mark
    ('Larger wings have more air resistance' gets both marks.)

TOTAL: 41 marks

FORCES IN ACTION

Recording teacher assessment using QCA Schemes of work

Class/year group: …………………… Teacher: ……………………………………

The majority of pupils have met the learning outcomes as stated in the medium-term plans from this QCA unit and they can:

- identify that weight is a force and is measured in newtons
- describe some situations in which there are two forces acting on an object and recognise that when the object is at rest the forces are balanced
- draw diagrams to illustrate forces acting on an object
- use a forcemeter accurately to measure forces
- present measurements in simple line graphs and identify patterns in these.

+

Some have made more progress and can also:

- describe and explain the motion of some familiar objects in terms of balanced or unbalanced forces.

Names or initials
(Include explanatory notes as necessary.)

−

Some have not made this much progress but can:

- identify weight as a force
- recognise that more than one force can act on an object
- use a forcemeter to measure forces and present measurements in tables.

Names or initials
(Include explanatory notes as necessary.)

The back of this sheet is on page 144.

FORCES IN ACTION

My concept map

Name ....

Look at the words below. Link the boxes together and label the lines, explaining your links.

You might want to cut the boxes out and arrange them yourself on a clean piece of paper.

You could draw your own concept map, using the same words.

| force |

| upthrust | | air resistance |

| water | | newtons |

| gravity |

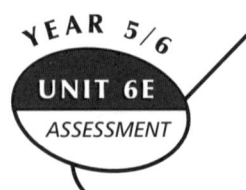

FORCES IN ACTION

What affects how quickly a spinner falls?

In your group, look at the children's ideas in the cartoon below.

Discuss their ideas.

Which do you agree with?

How could you test to see who is right?

I think that the more paperclips we have on the end, the faster the spinner will fall.

I think making the spinner out of different types of card and paper will affect it. I bet one made out of card stays up really well.

I think it will be the length of the wings that matters most. Long wings will be best.

HOW WE SEE THINGS

Pupil checklist

By the end of this unit:

I should know that:

- [ ] light travels from a source
- [ ] we see light sources because light travels from the source into our eyes
- [ ] light from an object can be reflected by a mirror
- [ ] the reflected light enters our eyes and we see the object
- [ ] when light is reflected, its direction changes
- [ ] shiny surfaces reflect light better than dull surfaces.

I should be able to:

- [ ] use what I know about light to explain my observations
- [ ] draw a straight line to show the path of a light ray, and include an arrow to show the direction of the ray
- [ ] make careful observations and comparisons
- [ ] record comparisons of how different surfaces reflect light
- [ ] draw conclusions from the comparisons I have made of light reflected from different surfaces
- [ ] identify factors that might affect the size and position of a shadow formed by an object
- [ ] investigate how one factor causes a shadow to change
- [ ] look for trends in results and see if any results do not fit the general pattern
- [ ] check measurements by repeating them
- [ ] recognise the difference between shadows and 'reflections'.

HOW WE SEE THINGS

Assessment questions

Name .... **Class** .... **Date** ....

1 Suppose you have a piece of black card with a small hole cut in the middle of it. You place the card in front of a torch. Then you look at the torch shining on a block of wood.

card with hole in centre

a) Using a ruler and a sharp pencil, draw rays of light on the diagram above, to show how a shadow forms on the screen.

(3)

b) Explain, in the space below, how the shadow from the block of wood forms.

....
....
....

(2)

c) What is the light source in the experiment above? ....

(1)

d) How would the experiment be different if the block were made of glass instead of wood?

....

(1)

Science Assessment Y5/6   © Lawrie Ryan, Nelson Thornes Ltd. 2002

2 a) Zoe looks at a pin in a mirror.

Use a ruler and a sharp pencil to draw a ray of light to show how Zoe sees the pin-head. Make sure you put arrows on the light ray to show which way the light travels.

pin

Zoe   mirror

(3)

b) Complete the sentence below by filling in the missing words.

The light from the pin is .... by the .... surface of the mirror.

(2)

c) What would Zoe see if the surface of the mirror were covered in paper?

....

(1)

d) Zoe moves the mirror so it is at a different angle, like this.

Describe where Zoe would have to move to, so that she could see the pin.

....

(1)

3 Some children were finding out what affects the size of a pencil's shadow.

They decided to see if changing the distance between the torch and the pencil made any difference.

They measured the height of the shadow on the wall.

a) What would they change in each of their tests?

....

(1)

b) The table of their results is shown below.

Distance between torch and pencil (cm)	Height of pencil's shadow (cm)
50	10
40	15
30	24
20	28
10	55

Use the grid on the next page to present these results on a graph.

Continued on next page

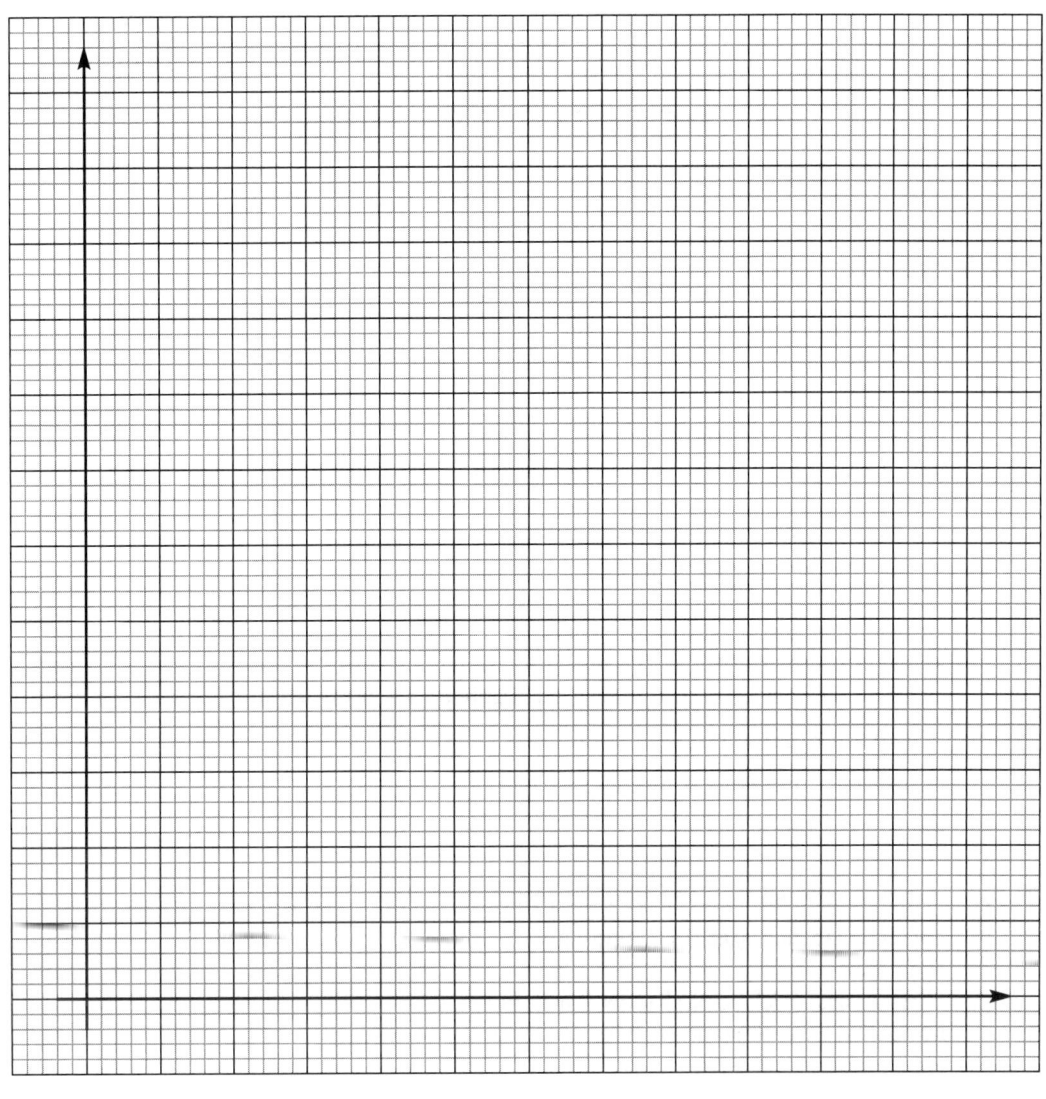

(6)

c) From your graph, what is the pattern?

   ....

   ....
   (2)

d) Draw a ring around the result on the graph that you think the group should check again.

   (1)

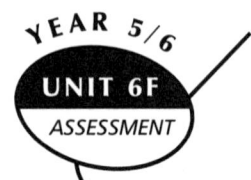

HOW WE SEE THINGS

Mark scheme

1	a)	Light rays from hole in card to wall	1 mark
		drawn with ruler	1 mark
		just touching tip of pencil.	1 mark
	b)	Light travels in straight lines.	1 mark
		Wood blocks rays of light (opaque) so it is dark behind it.	1 mark
	c)	torch	1 mark
	d)	no shadow (or very faint shadow)	1 mark
2	a)	Straight lines drawn with ruler	1 mark
		arrow(s) on ray pointing from pin-head to mirror to eye	1 mark
		angle of ray coming in to the mirror roughly equal to ray leaving.	1 mark
	b)	reflected, shiny/silver(y)	2 marks
	c)	no reflection/nothing/no pin (allow paper)	1 mark
	d)	down(wards)/or to right	1 mark
3	a)	distance between the torch and the pencil	1 mark
	b)	correctly labelled axes, including units	1 mark
		even scale	1 mark
		Vertical axis: 'Height of shadow (cm)' and horizontal axis: 'Distance between torch and pencil (cm)'.	1 mark
		Points plotted correctly	2 marks
		and joined by line.	1 mark
	c)	The greater the distance between torch (light source) and pencil (object), the shorter the shadow (or vice versa). (Only 1 mark for specific example, e.g. 'When the distance between the torch and the shadow is large, the shadow is short (small).')	2 marks
	d)	ring around 20, 28	1 mark

TOTAL: 24 marks

YEAR 5/6 UNIT 6F ASSESSMENT

HOW WE SEE THINGS

Recording teacher assessment using QCA Schemes of work

Class/year group: .... Teacher: ....

The majority of pupils have met the learning outcomes as stated in the medium-term plans from this QCA unit and they can:

- recognise that light travels from a source, that when it is blocked a shadow is formed and when it hits a shiny surface it is reflected
- recognise that light sources are seen when light from them enters the eyes
- make careful measurements of shadows and represent them in a line graph.

+	−
Some have made more progress and can also: • explain the differences between shadow formation and reflection in terms of the path of light.	**Some have not made this much progress but can:** • recognise that when light is blocked a shadow is formed, and that reflections can be seen in shiny surfaces • make measurements and present them in a table.
Names or initials (Include explanatory notes as necessary.)	**Names or initials** (Include explanatory notes as necessary.)

The back of this sheet is on page 144.

Science Assessment Y5/6   © Lawrie Ryan, Nelson Thornes Ltd. 2002

YEAR 5/6 UNIT 6F ASSESSMENT

HOW WE SEE THINGS

My concept map

Name ....

Look at the words below. Link the boxes together and label the lines, explaining your links.

You might want to cut the boxes out and arrange them yourself on a clean piece of paper.

You could draw your own concept map, using the same words.

| light rays | shadows |

| light source | shiny |

| opaque | reflect |

| mirror |

Science Assessment Y5/6   © Lawrie Ryan, Nelson Thornes Ltd. 2002

HOW WE SEE THINGS

Complete the diagram

Draw a light ray on the diagram below to show how Jake sees the book.

Use arrows to show which way the light ray travels.

CHANGING CIRCUITS

Pupil checklist

By the end of this unit:

I should know that:

- [ ] the brightness of a bulb in a circuit can be changed
- [ ] the speed of a motor in a circuit can be changed
- [ ] I must take care to choose the right bulb or motor to put into a circuit if they are not to burn out
- [ ] I can use symbols to make a circuit diagram to show a circuit
- [ ] the brightness of a bulb can be changed by changing wires in a circuit.

I should be able to:

- [ ] draw a circuit diagram to represent my experiments
- [ ] follow a circuit diagram to construct a circuit
- [ ] suggest a question about bulbs to investigate
- [ ] plan how to test my question about what affects the brightness of a bulb
- [ ] carry out fair comparisons between circuits
- [ ] use my results to draw conclusions
- [ ] use my knowledge of electrical circuits to explain my observations.

Science Assessment Y5/6   © Lawrie Ryan, Nelson Thornes Ltd. 2002

CHANGING CIRCUITS

Assessment questions

Name .... Class .... Date ....

1 All the cells in this question have the same voltage.

In which of the circuits below will the bulbs light up?

Put a tick under each one that works and a cross under each one that won't work.

a)
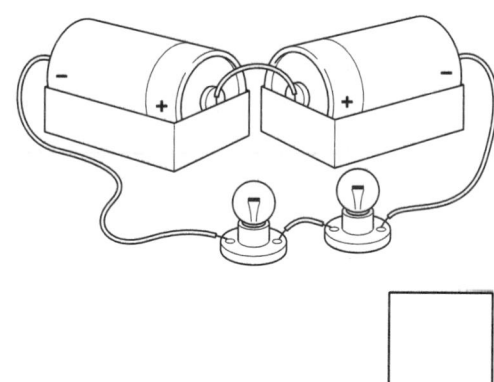

b)
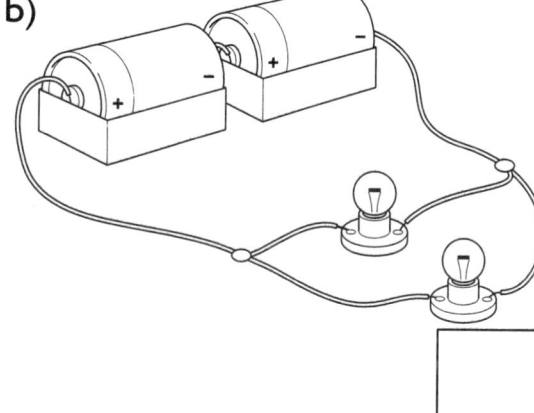

c)
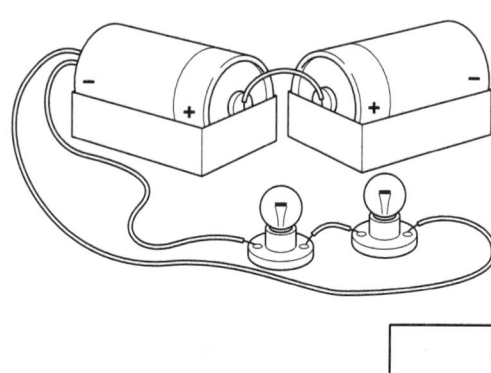

d)
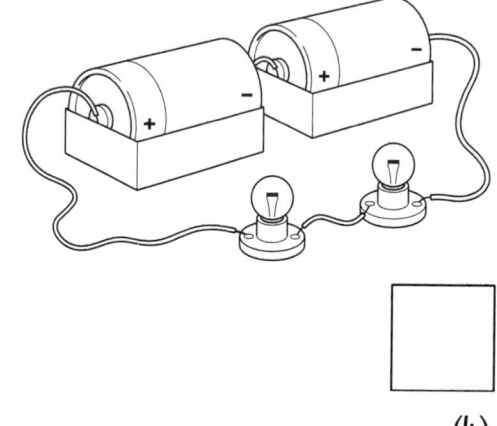

(4)

2 a) Draw the symbol for a cell in this box.

b) Draw the symbol for a wire in this box.

c) Draw the symbol for a switch in this box.

d) Draw the symbol for a bulb in this box.

(4)

e) Draw a circuit diagram to show a cell, a bulb and a switch in a circuit.
The switch should be turned off.

(4)

f) Explain why the bulb does not light up in your circuit in e) as drawn.

....

....

(2)

3 a) In which of these **three** circuits will the bulb shine most brightly? Tick the box by the circuit you choose, then complete the sentence.

☐ circuit A   ☐ circuit B   ☐ circuit C   (1)

This shows that the .... , the brighter the bulb.
(1)

b) In which of these **three** circuits will the bulb shine brightest? Tick the box by the circuit you choose, then complete the sentence below.

☐ circuit A   ☐ circuit B   ☐ circuit C   (1)s

This shows that the .... , the brighter the bulb.
(1)

c) A group of children were given some thin wire to see if its length made any difference to the brightness of the bulb.

i) Name **two** things that they should keep the same to make fair comparisons.

.... and ....
(2)

ii) What do you think that the group found out?

....

....
(2)

Science Assessment Y5/6   © Lawrie Ryan, Nelson Thornes Ltd. 2002

CHANGING CIRCUITS

Mark scheme

1. a) ✗ — 1 mark
   b) ✓ — 1 mark
   c) ✗ — 1 mark
   d) ✓ — 1 mark

2. a) —|⊢— (cell symbol) — 1 mark

   b) ——— (wire) — 1 mark

   c) switch symbol (open) — 1 mark

   d) bulb symbol — 1 mark

   e) complete circuit with cell, switch and bulb — 4 marks

   (1 mark for each correct symbol, 1 mark for complete circuit)

   f) Not a complete circuit/gap in circuit — 1 mark
      so electricity cannot flow. — 1 mark

3. a) circuit C — 1 mark
      the higher the voltage/the more cells (allow more batteries) — 1 mark
   b) circuit A — 1 mark
      the thicker the wire — 1 mark
   c) number of cells (allow batteries) — 1 mark
      number of bulbs — 1 mark
   d) The longer the wire, the dimmer the bulb or vice versa. — 2 marks
      (only 1 mark for specific case, for example,
      'The long wire gave a dim bulb.')

TOTAL: 22 marks

CHANGING CIRCUITS

Recording teacher assessment using QCA Schemes of work

Class/year group: …………………… **Teacher:** ……………………………………

The majority of pupils have met the learning outcomes as stated in the medium-term plans from this QCA unit and they can:

- suggest ways of changing the brightness of a bulb in a circuit
- use conventional symbols to draw circuit diagrams, and construct circuits from conventional circuit diagrams
- set up a circuit which can be used to investigate an idea and use knowledge about electrical conductors and insulators to answer questions about circuits.

+

Some have made more progress and can also:

- interpret more complex circuit diagrams and describe differences between fuse wire and wires usually used for circuits.

Names or initials
(Include explanatory notes as necessary.)

−

Some have not made this much progress but can:

- recognise conventional symbols for some electrical components and construct some working circuits with specified components.

Names or initials
(Include explanatory notes as necessary.)

The back of this sheet is on page 144.

Science Assessment Y5/6   © Lawrie Ryan, Nelson Thornes Ltd. 2002

CHANGING CIRCUITS

My concept map

Name ....

Look at the words below. Link the boxes together and label the lines, explaining your links.

You might want to cut the boxes out and arrange them yourself on a clean piece of paper.

You could draw your own concept map, using the same words.

| electricity |

| cell | | bulbs |

| wires | | motor |

| buzzer | circuit |

Science Assessment Y5/6   © Lawrie Ryan, Nelson Thornes Ltd. 2002

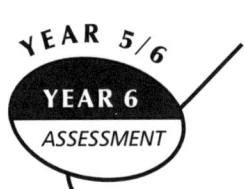

END-OF-YEAR ASSESSMENT QUESTIONS

Name .... Class .... Date ....

1 A farmer adds some fertiliser to his soil.

a) Explain how the plants take in the useful materials from the fertiliser.

....

....
(2)

b) Besides nutrients, what else must a plant take in to make new material and grow?

.... and ....
(2)

c) In which part of a plant does it make its own 'food for growth'?

....
(1)

d) Which one of these statements is true?

Tick the box by the correct answer.

☐ Plants eat soil which is turned into new plant material.

☐ Plants absorb small amounts of nutrients from the soil to help them grow.

☐ Plants only use soil to anchor themselves down.
(1)

2 Lots of people like home-made bread.

a) Which micro-organism do we add to the bread dough-mixture to make it rise?

....
(1)

b) What does the micro-organism feed on to make the mixture rise?

....
(1)

c) What other conditions do we need for the bread dough-mixture to rise?

....
(1)

d) Write down **two** other foods that are made using micro-organisms.

1 ....

2 ....
(2)

3 Some children were finding out which type of sugar dissolves most quickly. They tried to make their test as fair as possible.

    a) Write down **three** things that they should keep the same in each test.

        1 ....

        2 ....

        3 ....

        (3)

    b) The table of their results is shown below..

Type of sugar	Time to dissolve (seconds)
brown	150
granulated	120
cube	300
caster	40

Use the grid below to present these results in a graph.

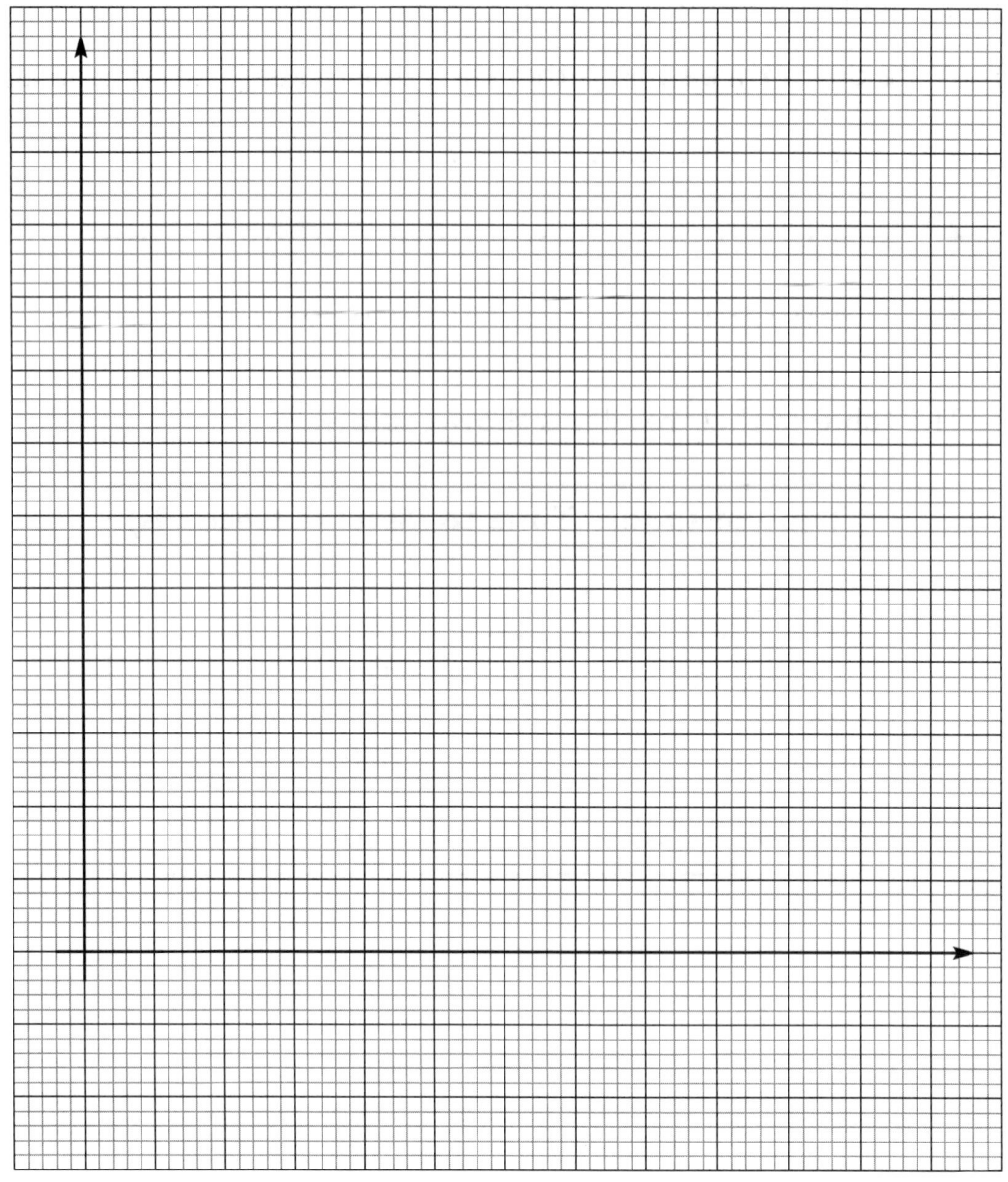

(7)

c) Which sugar dissolves most quickly? ....

(1)

d) How could the group have made their results more reliable?

....

(1)

e) How could the group get some sugar back from the solution?

....

(1)

4 a) Look at the picture of the gas cooker below.

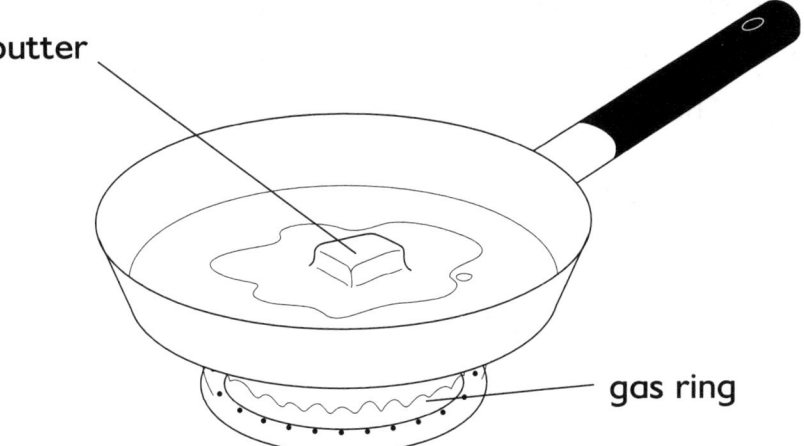

Use the ideas in picture to describe the difference between reversible an irreversible changes.

....

....

....

....

....

....

(4)

b) Some salt in the kitchen gets mixed accidentally with sand. Describe a method you could use to get pure salt back again.

....

....

....

....

....

(3)

5 Some children were investigating paper spinners. They decided to see if the length of the wings affects how long the spinner takes to fall. They repeated each test three times. Their table of results is given below.

a) Work out the average (mean) time for the spinner when the wings are 5 cm long. Put your answer in the table.

Length of wings (cm)	Time for spinner to hit the floor (seconds)			
	First try	Second try	Third try	Mean (average)
2	1.25	1.33	0.78	1.12
3	1.57	1.38	1.34	1.43
4	1.76	1.89	1.60	1.75
5	2.09	1.98	2.02	

(1)

b) Why was it a good idea to repeat their readings?

....
(1)

c) Which reading would you have least confidence in? Explain why.

....

....
(2)

d) The graph of the first three tests is shown on the right.

Plot the last point on the graph and finish off the line.

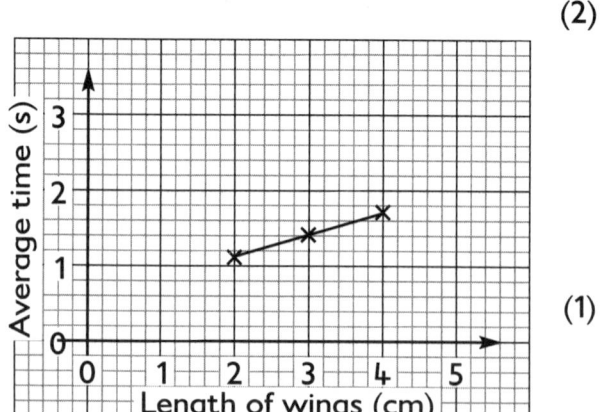

(1)

e) Explain how the time it takes a spinner to fall depends on the length of its wings.

....

....
(2)

6 Arran set up this experiment to investigate shadows. He changed the distance between the torch and the pencil. This is his table of results.

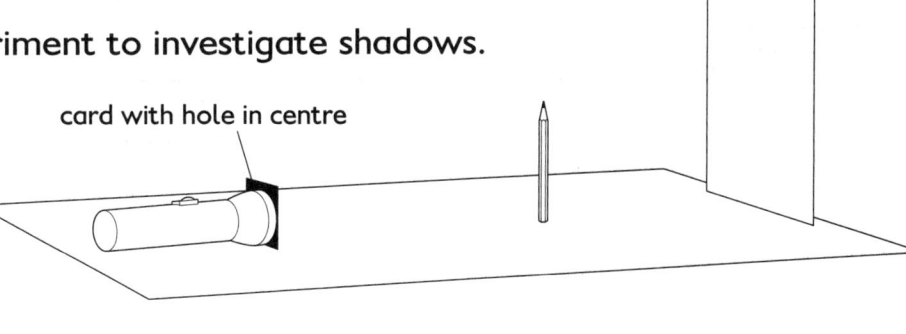

Distance between torch and pencil (cm)	Height of shadow (cm)
10	65
20	34
30	26
40	20
50	18

a) Use the grid to draw a graph to show his results. Name the axes. (9)

b) How does the height of the shadow depend on the distance between the torch and pencil?

....
(2)

7 a) In which of these **three** circuits, A, B or C, will the bulb shine most brightly? Tick the box by the circuit you choose.

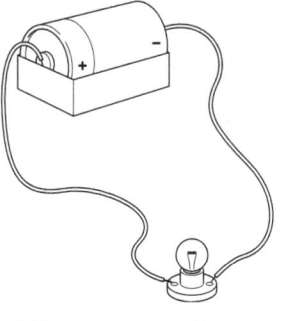 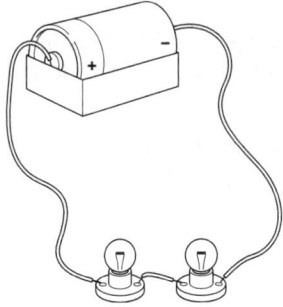 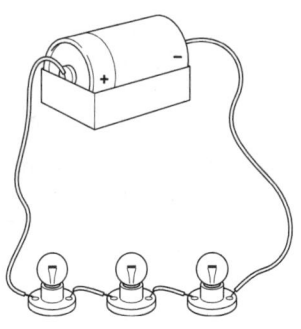

☐ circuit A   ☐ circuit B   ☐ circuit C
(1)

b) How does the number of bulbs in the circuit affect their brightness?

....
(2)

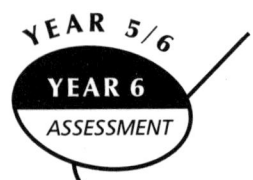

END OF YEAR ASSESSMENT QUESTIONS

Mark scheme

1	a)	dissolves in water	1 mark
		taken in/absorbed through roots	1 mark
	b)	air (carbon dioxide) and water	2 marks
	c)	leaves	1 mark
	d)	Plants absorb small amounts of nutrients from the soil to help them grow.	1 mark
2	a)	yeast	1 mark
	b)	sugar	1 mark
	c)	warmth	1 mark
	d)	two examples, e.g. yoghurt/cheese	2 marks
3	a)	three factors to control, for example temperature, rate of stirring, volume (amount) of water, mass (amount) of sugar	3 marks
	b)	1 mark for each correctly plotted point	6 marks
		points joined with line	1 mark
	c)	caster	1 mark
	d)	by repeating the experiment	1 mark
	e)	Evaporate off the water.	1 mark
4	a)	Look for these points:	
		Butter melts and	1 mark
		can easily turn back to solid butter – reversible change.	1 mark
		Gas burns,	1 mark
		making new materials that cannot be changed back to gas we started with – irreversible.	1 mark
	b)	Add water (and stir).	1 mark
		Filter the mixture.	1 mark
		Evaporate off the water.	1 mark
5	a)	2.03	1 mark
	b)	Because the times were so short it is difficult to be accurate.	1 mark
	c)	The first set	1 mark
		because they have the biggest differences/shortest time gives biggest error in timings	1 mark
	d)	Point plotted correctly	1 mark
	e)	The longer the wings, the longer it takes the spinner to fall (only 1 mark for specific example, e.g. 'With long wings it takes the spinner a long time to fall.')	2 marks
6	a)	Vertical axis chosen for 'Height of shadow', horizontal for 'Distance between torch and pencil'.	1 mark
		Both axes labelled correctly, including units.	1 mark
		Even scale chosen.	1 mark
		1 mark for each point correctly plotted.	5 marks
		Points joined by line (or line of best fit).	1 mark
	b)	The closer the torch is to the pencil, the higher/taller/bigger the shadow. (only 1 mark for specific example, e.g. 'When the torch and pencil are close together the shadow is high/tall/big.')	2 marks
7	a)	A	1 mark
	b)	The more bulbs, the dimmer they are, or vice versa. (only 1 mark for specific example, e.g. 'With a lot bulbs in a circuit, they are dim.')	2 marks

TOTAL: 52 marks

SUMMARY OF ATTAINMENT IN QCA UNITS

Years 5 and 6

Key: a blank box means that children have met the end of unit expectations for most children as stated in the QCA scheme of work

+ means that children progress beyond these expectations

− means that children do not meet the expectations for most children

Name	Unit													level
	5A	5B	5C	5D	5E	5F	6A	6B	6C	6D	6E	6F	6G	

Science Assessment Y5/6   © Lawrie Ryan, Nelson Thornes Ltd. 2002

RECORD OF ATTAINMENT

+

Names or initials
(Include explanatory notes as necessary.)

–

Names or initials
(Include explanatory notes as necessary.)

Other notes